Charts

OF

Modern and Postmodern Church History

Books in the Zondervan*Charts* Series

OF

Modern and Postmodern Church History

John D. Hannah

GRAND RAPIDS, MICHIGAN 49530 USA

ZONDERVAN™

Charts of Modern and Postmodern Church History
Copyright © 2004 by John David Hannah

Requests for information should be addressed to:
Zondervan, *Grand Rapids, Michigan 49530*

Library of Congress Cataloging-in-Publication Data

Hannah, John D.
    Charts of modern and postmodern church history / John D. Hannah.
        p. cm.
    ISBN 0-310-23530-8
    1. Church history—Chronology—Charts, diagrams, etc.   I. Title.   II. Series.
    BR149.H333 2004
    270.8'02'02—dc22

                                                                    2004009422

Interior design by Angela Moulter

Printed in the United States of America

04 05 06 07 08 09 / ❖ VG/ 10 9 8 7 6 5 4 3 2 1

Dedication

This volume is dedicated to over three decades of students at Dallas Seminary. They not only made teaching a delight, they caused me to think deeply about the art of teaching. I was forced to answer the questions: How do students learn? What is the nature of learning? How are concepts conveyed through invisible symbols such as speech from one mind to another? How do visual symbols facilitate the learning process? How can they be used most effectively in the classroom?

It is with love for God, expressed in the execution of a calling, and an immense desire to maximize student learning potential that the final volume in this Zondervan*Charts* series-within-a-series is published. To the students of Dallas Theological Seminary, Dallas, Texas, I thank you for enriching my life through teaching me something of the art of classroom communication.

112107

Acknowledgments

The successful completion of a project is never the work of a single individual. It takes a variety of people with specialized talents. Some of the many who made this volume possible, I'd like to acknowledge here:

The visualization of concepts involves more than ideas; it takes graphic talents and an educational environment willing to invest the time and expertise to enhance a teacher's effectiveness. I thank the boards and administration of Dallas Theological Seminary for their commitment to faculty classroom development. Most particularly, I owe a great debt to the AV department, directed by Don Regier and staffed by self-giving people who listen to ideas and bring them to life for classroom use. I thank Mary Nees, who painstakingly assisted me when I was a young teacher, and now to Linda Tomczak who is equally adept.

The staff of Mosher Library, particularly Jeff Webster, has consistently provided help and counsel, often dropping other duties to assist me. The secretary in the Theological Studies department, Beth Motley, is an unsung hero. In my judgment, behind every teacher who has any measure of success is an excellent secretary. Further, two graduate students—David Largent and Blake Altman—have been of special assistance with this project. Friends are forged through common endeavors and these have become mine.

I want to thank Zondervan for their commitment to seeing this multivolume project to completion. The editor of this volume was Greg Clouse, a former student of mine years ago. He proved a delight to me personally with his wisdom, expertise, and love. He is truly a tribute to the grace of his Lord and a friend to me.

A special thanks goes to my wife, Carolyn Ruth Hannah. She is married to an obsessive-compulsive. It has not always been spiritually conducive to her that I am so preoccupied with tasks. However, her gentle recognition of my calling as a teacher and willingness to sacrifice in the pursuit of that calling is a contribution beyond words. I thank her for her dedication to my calling before God to serve his church in the classroom.

Contents

Charts of Modern and Postmodern Church History

The value of history has fallen on difficult times in contemporary culture. Postmoderns have demonstrated a tendency to disregard the past as a useless and even debilitating relic, something akin to unwanted dreams and painful experiences. Learning from the collective wisdom of the ages seems of little value in an era where technology and the sciences receive the most support through government funding while the arts and humanities are marginalized. We seem determined to improve our outward circumstances while allowing the inner life to decay. Great literature is not read and cherished, cultural values are nullified through the ever-changing excitement of the merely transitory, and life is tyrannized by captivating trivia. A society without a knowledge of its past is one without hope, cursed with the perception that an endless array of passing fads is meaningful. What we seem to prize most is the stuff of future garage sales, the emptiness of preoccupation with athleticism, the spiral of increased debt, and the phantom of deep relationships shattered by broken promises.

At least in part, the contemporary church seems to have imbibed the culture more than resisted its largely unbiblical values. This can be seen in the lack of awareness many Christians have of their heritage. With some sense of discomfort they may be enticed to articulate a vague awareness of Martin Luther or John Calvin, yet there seems to be little understanding that the Christian faith draws on a rich heritage that is centuries in its development. Part of the problem, if truth be told, is that in many of our educational institutions and churches Christians are not being grounded in their heritage.

This brings me to the purpose for this third and final volume in the series on the history of the Christian church. Before one bemoans the situation too incessantly, he ought to try to do something about it. What I've provided are tools for the teaching of our heritage: various charts, diagrams, and maps, together with explanatory captions, unfolding the history of the church. Included with the book is a CD-ROM PowerPoint® presentation, which enhances the use of each teaching tool.

In using this third volume, the teacher and student must be reminded that the history of the church cannot be neatly divided and compartmentalized. Movements have a context that precedes their appearance, and this is important to grasp if we are to gain a more accurate understanding. The microscope of details must be placed in the telescopic perspective of broad events. Simply put, movements and events (even people) have a prehistory that, at least to some degree, helps us to understand them. Therefore, it's important to view this volume in the context of the previous one. The modern and the postmodern eras can most fully be appreciated when seen in the light of the rise and disintegration of the Enlightenment.

THE NATIONAL PERIOD OF AMERICAN CHURCH HISTORY

Religious Change in
New England: Theological
Divisions within Congregationalism

Congregationalism in America

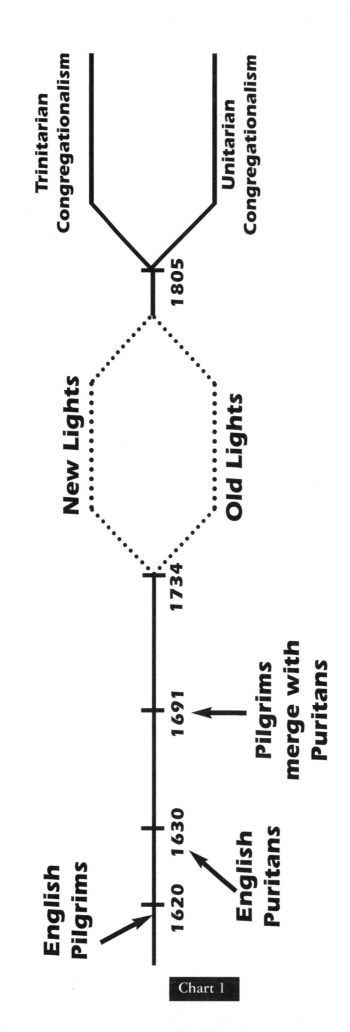

English Pilgrims 1620

1630 **English Puritans**

1691 **Pilgrims merge with Puritans**

1734

New Lights

Old Lights

1805

Trinitarian Congregationalism

Unitarian Congregationalism

Chart 1

As a result of the Enlightenment, the Congregational Church was rocked by theological controversy in the eighteenth and early nineteenth centuries. First, factions developed over the Great Awakening, the so-called New Lights viewing the revival positively and the so-called Old Lights viewing it quite the opposite. Ultimately, issues over a successor to the Hollis Chair of Divinity at Harvard College divided the denomination into Trinitarians and Unitarians.

Developments within Nineteenth-Century American Theology

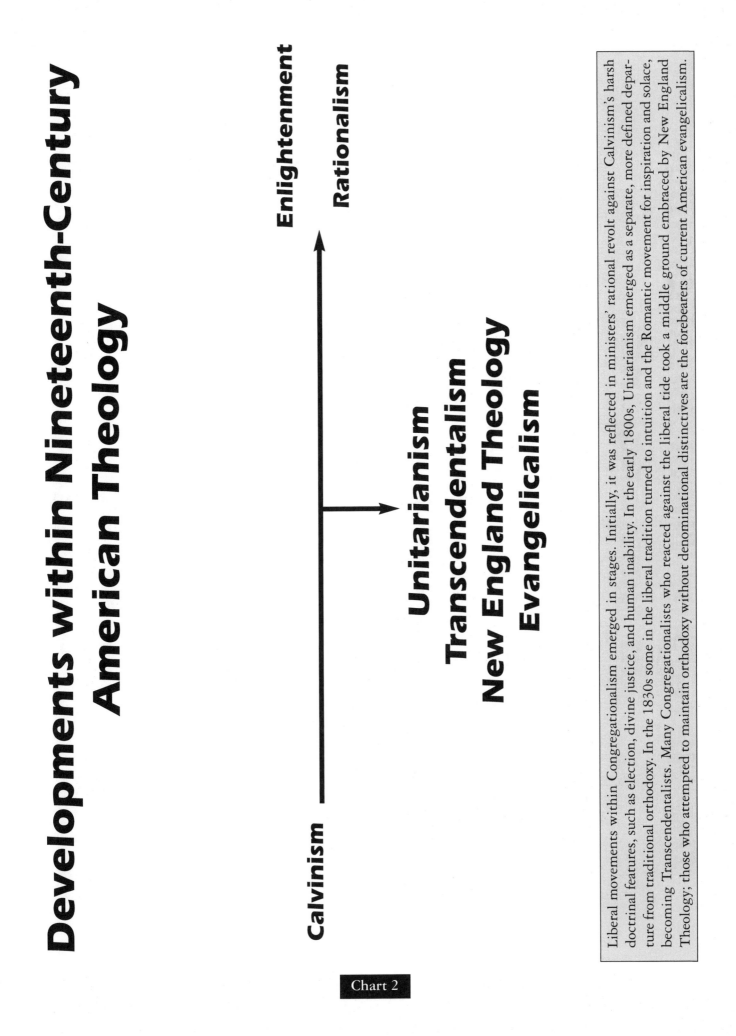

Enlightenment

Rationalism

Unitarianism
Transcendentalism
New England Theology
Evangelicalism

Calvinism

Chart 2

Liberal movements within Congregationalism emerged in stages. Initially, it was reflected in ministers' rational revolt against Calvinism's harsh doctrinal features, such as election, divine justice, and human inability. In the early 1800s, Unitarianism emerged as a separate, more defined departure from traditional orthodoxy. In the 1830s some in the liberal tradition turned to intuition and the Romantic movement for inspiration and solace, becoming Transcendentalists. Many Congregationalists who reacted against the liberal tide took a middle ground embraced by New England Theology; those who attempted to maintain orthodoxy without denominational distinctives are the forebearers of current American evangelicalism.

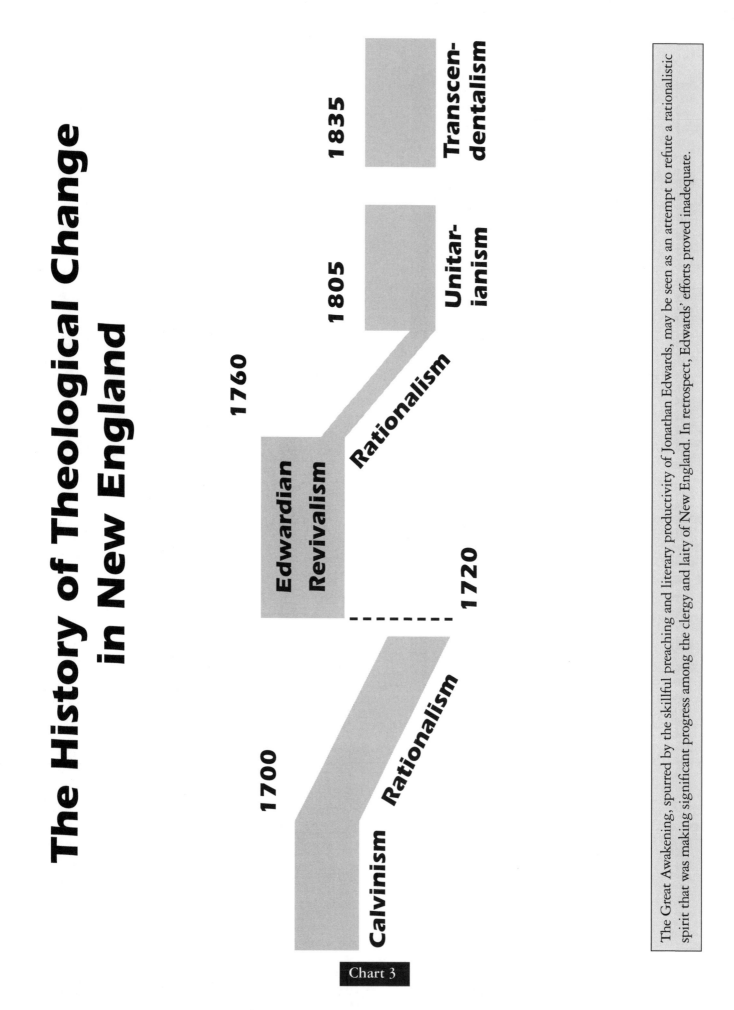

The History of Theological Change in New England

Chart 3

1700 — Calvinism

Rationalism

1720

1760 — Edwardian Revivalism

Rationalism

1805 — Unitarianism

1835 — Transcendentalism

The Great Awakening, spurred by the skillful preaching and literary productivity of Jonathan Edwards, may be seen as an attempt to refute a rationalistic spirit that was making significant progress among the clergy and laity of New England. In retrospect, Edwards' efforts proved inadequate.

The Rise of Unitarianism in America

Rationalism

Unitarianism

Transcendentalism

Introductory
Period

Moderate
Period

Mature
Period

1805

1835

Charles
Chauncy

William
Channing

Ralph Waldo
Emerson

Chart 4

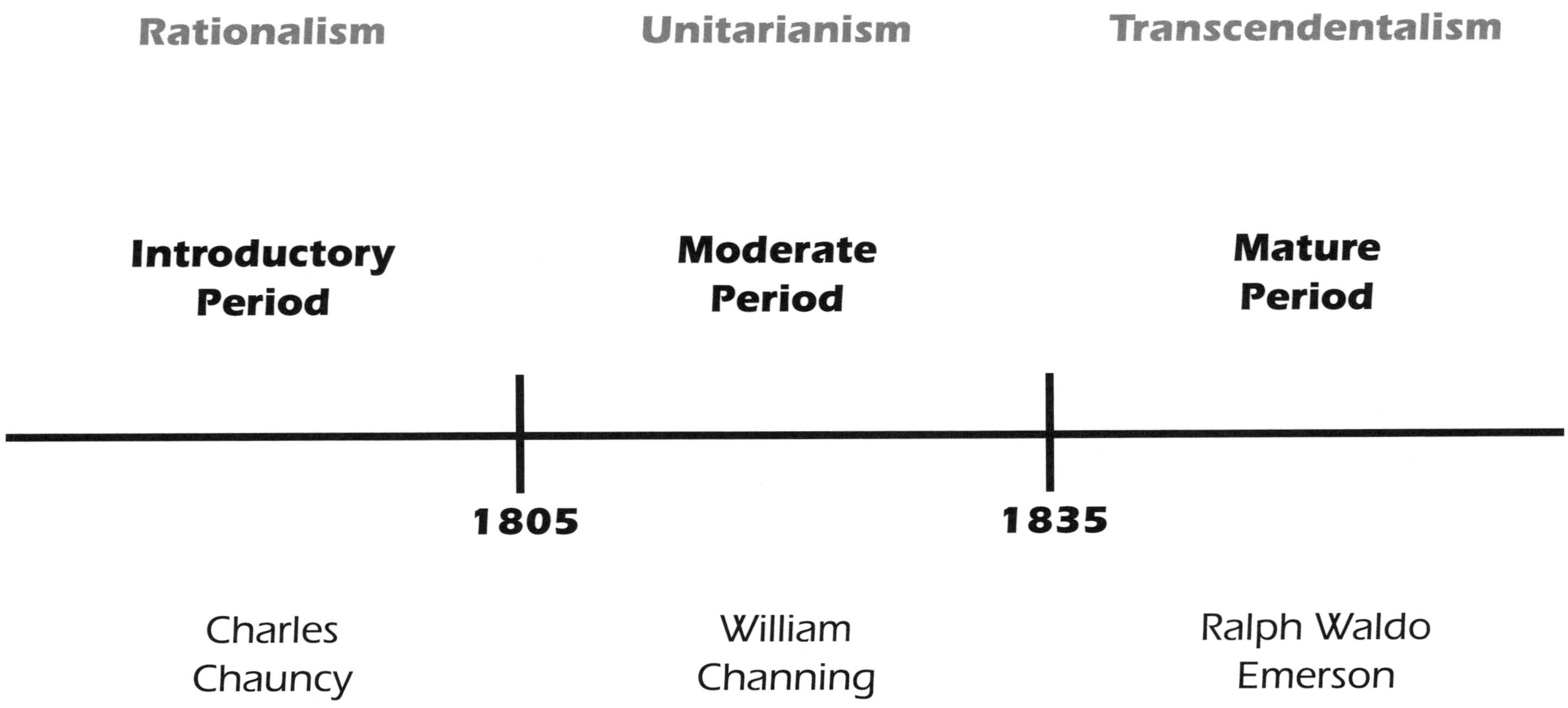

Each phase of the revolt against orthodoxy in New England may be said to have had a representative. Charles Chauncy's clash with Jonathan Edwards reflected the initial phase. William Channing's "Unitarian Christianity" address (1819) defined the second phase and Ralph Waldo Emerson's "Divinity School Address" (1838) the last phase.

The History of Unitarianism in America

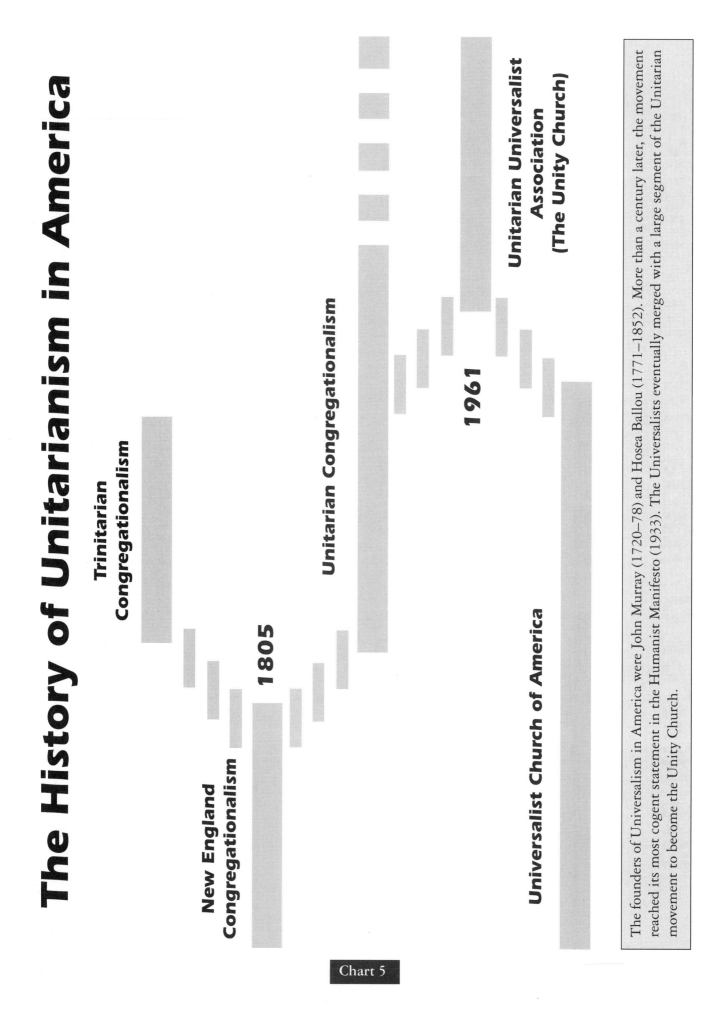

Trinitarian Congregationalism

Unitarian Congregationalism

New England Congregationalism

1805

1961

Unitarian Universalist Association (The Unity Church)

Universalist Church of America

The founders of Universalism in America were John Murray (1720–78) and Hosea Ballou (1771–1852). More than a century later, the movement reached its most cogent statement in the Humanist Manifesto (1933). The Universalists eventually merged with a large segment of the Unitarian movement to become the Unity Church.

Chart 5

Orthodoxy, Unitarianism, and Transcendentalism: A Comparison

	ORTHODOXY	UNITARIANISM	TRANSCEN-DENTALISM
PHILOSOPHICAL ORIENTATION:	Realism	Realism	Idealism
EPISTEMOLOGY:	Reformation Empiricism Rationalism	Empiricism Rationalism Reformation	Intuition
GOD:	Theistic Plural Personal	Theistic Single Personal	Panentheistic Impersonal
MEDIUM OF REVELATION:	Supernatural Natural	Natural Supernatural	Natural
PERSON OF CHRIST:	God/Man	Archetypical Man	Man
NATURE OF SIN:	Derived and Personal Depravity, Moral Inability	Personal Depravity, Moral Ability	Personal Depravity, Moral Ability
ATONEMENT:	Penal	Exemplary	None
SOURCES:	Reformation	Reformation	Romanticism

The Unitarian movement has an affinity with Congregational orthodoxy from which it developed. However, Unitarianism proposed such contrary interpretations of Christianity that it lost its essence and retained only its moral affiliations. Transcendentalism, while rooted in Unitarianism, went beyond the pale of Christian orthodoxy.

Chart 6

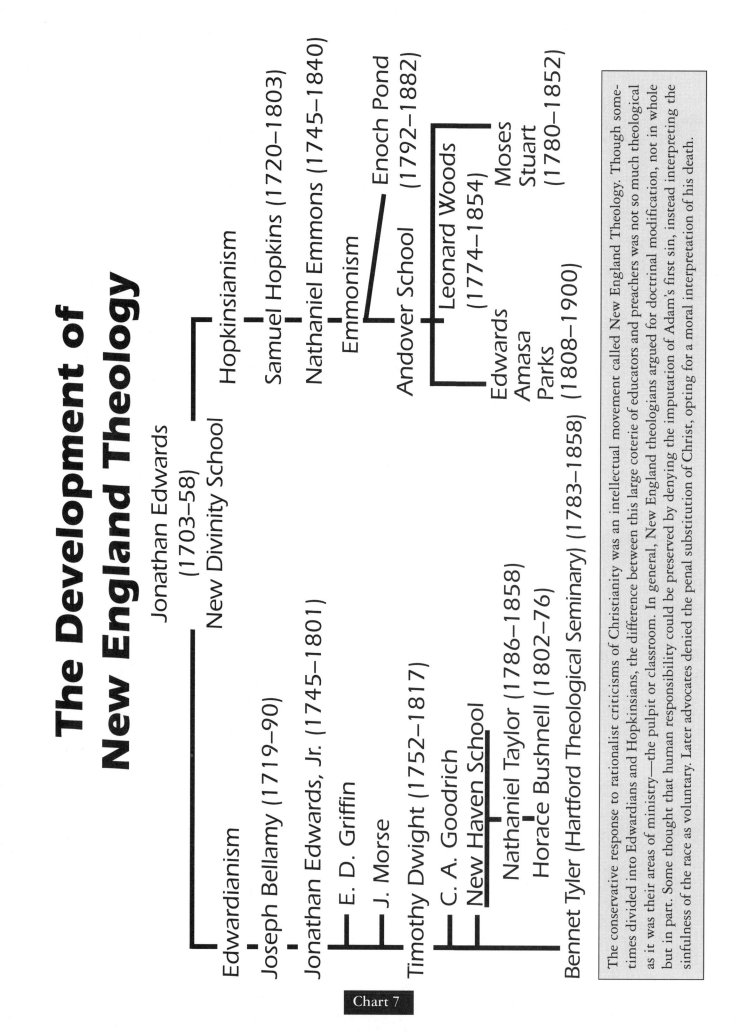

The Development of New England Theology

Jonathan Edwards (1703–58)

New Divinity School

Edwardianism

Joseph Bellamy (1719–90)

Jonathan Edwards, Jr. (1745–1801)

E. D. Griffin

J. Morse

Timothy Dwight (1752–1817)

C. A. Goodrich

New Haven School

Nathaniel Taylor (1786–1858)

Horace Bushnell (1802–76)

Bennet Tyler (Hartford Theological Seminary) (1783–1858)

Hopkinsianism

Samuel Hopkins (1720–1803)

Nathaniel Emmons (1745–1840)

Emmonism

Enoch Pond (1792–1882)

Andover School

Leonard Woods (1774–1854)

Moses Stuart (1780–1852)

Edwards Amasa Parks (1808–1900)

The conservative response to rationalist criticisms of Christianity was an intellectual movement called New England Theology. Though sometimes divided into Edwardians and Hopkinsians, the difference between this large coterie of educators and preachers was not so much theological as it was their areas of ministry—the pulpit or classroom. In general, New England theologians argued for doctrinal modification, not in whole but in part. Some thought that human responsibility could be preserved by denying the imputation of Adam's first sin, instead interpreting the sinfulness of the race as voluntary. Later advocates denied the penal substitution of Christ, opting for a moral interpretation of his death.

Chart 7

The Second Great Awakening, the Rise of Seminaries, and the Protestant Missionary Movement

The Eastern Phase of the Second Great Awakening: The Colleges

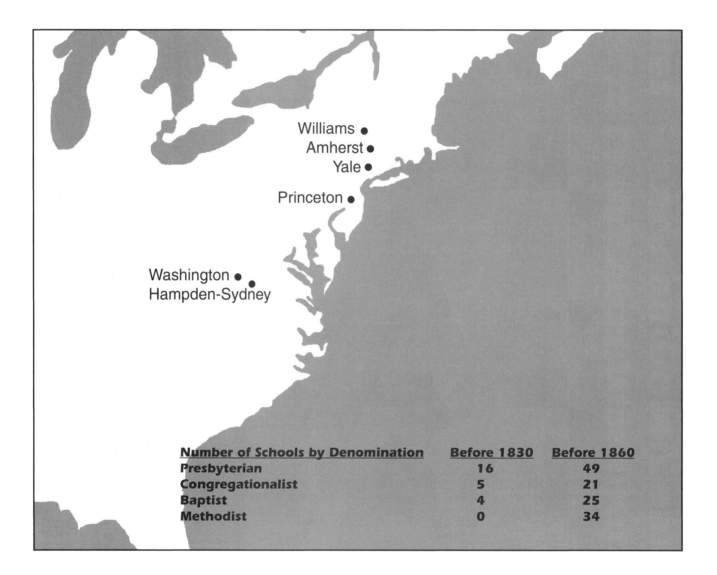

Williams •
Amherst •
Yale •

Princeton •

Washington • •
Hampden-Sydney

Number of Schools by Denomination	Before 1830	Before 1860
Presbyterian	16	49
Congregationalist	5	21
Baptist	4	25
Methodist	0	34

The Second Great Awakening appeared in the new nation between the 1780s and the early decades of the nineteenth century. In the East, spiritual awakenings swept the colleges that had suffered the loss of religious fervor through the rise of rationalism. Among these were Williams and Amherst in Massachusetts, Yale in Connecticut, Princeton in New Jersey, and Washington and Hampden-Sydney in Virginia. As a result, there was a massive resurgence of Christianity and an increase in educational institutions as more and more discovered the ministry enough to want to participate in it.

Chart 8

The Rural Phase of the Second Great Awakening: Camp Meetings

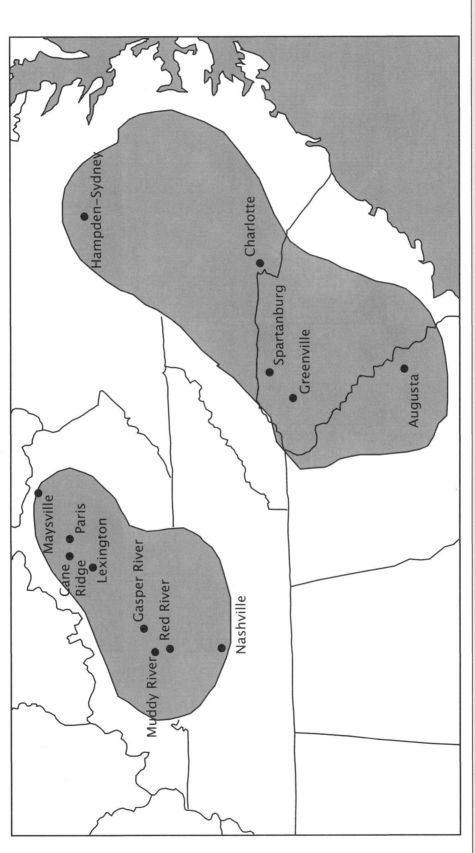

Maysville
Paris
Cane Ridge
Lexington
Gasper River
Red River
Muddy River
Nashville

Hampden-Sydney
Charlotte
Spartanburg
Greenville
Augusta

In the interior portions of the nation, the awakening was characterized by the invention of the camp meeting, a technique credited to Presbyterian minister James McGready (c. 1758–1817). Designed to bring the sparse population together in group gatherings, preachers from a variety of denominations often participated. The largest of the camp meetings was at Cane Ridge, Kentucky, in 1801 under Barton Stone (1772–1844). Circuit riders also roamed the frontier by horseback to preach and distribute Bibles.

Chart 9

History of the Restoration Movement (The Christian Church)

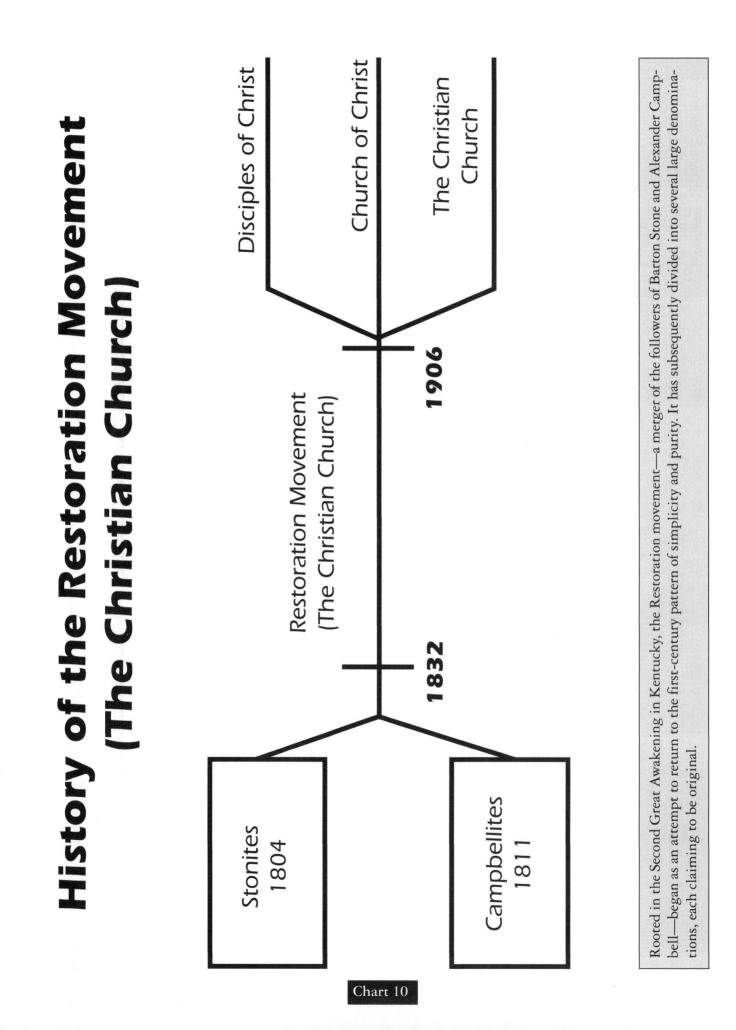

Disciples of Christ

Church of Christ

The Christian Church

1906

Restoration Movement
(The Christian Church)

1832

Stonites
1804

Campbellites
1811

Chart 10

Rooted in the Second Great Awakening in Kentucky, the Restoration movement—a merger of the followers of Barton Stone and Alexander Campbell—began as an attempt to return to the first-century pattern of simplicity and purity. It has subsequently divided into several large denominations, each claiming to be original.

Changes in Gospel Preaching: The Great Awakenings Compared

	FIRST GREAT AWAKENING	SECOND GREAT AWAKENING
Nature	Proclamation, theocentric	Persuasion, anthropocentric
Illustrations	Biblical, to illustrate	Stories, to convince
Application	Wait for mercy	Immediate decision
Preachers' View of Congregation	Should have faith . . . but can't (inability)	Can have faith . . . . but won't (stubbornness)

As the new nation was forged upon the political theory that government is formed through the consent of the governed, religious preference was cast in the same light. It was now a personal choice. This changed the nature of the content and appeal of the gospel. The message was fashioned to secure a vote of confidence, the appeal was universalized, and illustrations were meant to move one to a decision.

Chart 11

The Rise of Theological Seminaries

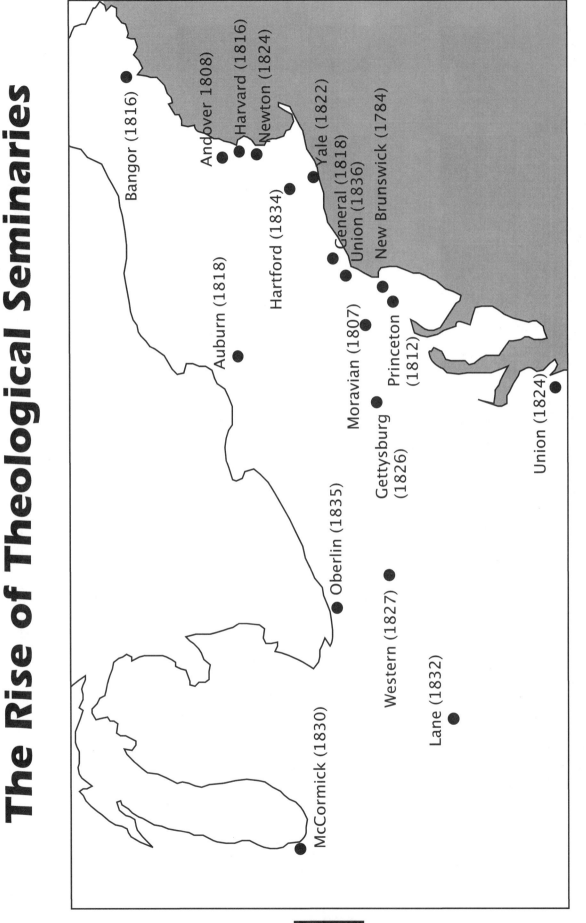

Bangor (1816)

Andover 1808

Harvard (1816)

Newton (1824)

Yale (1822)

Auburn (1818)

Hartford (1834)

General (1818)

Union (1836)

New Brunswick (1784)

Moravian (1807)

Princeton (1812)

Gettysburg (1826)

Oberlin (1835)

Western (1827)

Lane (1832)

McCormick (1830)

Union (1824)

In the new nation, the preparation of clergy gradually shifted away from the colleges to the seminaries. Seminaries emerged to provide a competently trained ministry for the churches. The Congregationalists and Presbyterians led the way in this educational endeavor.

Chart 12

The Birth of the
Modern Missions Movement

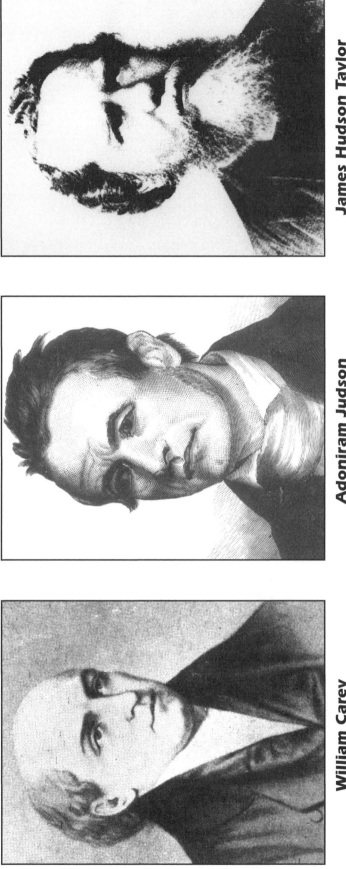

William Carey
(1761–1834)

Adoniram Judson
(1788–1850)

James Hudson Taylor
(1832–1905)

William Carey (1761–1834) has been recognized as the father of the English-speaking, foreign missions movement. In 1792 the Particular Baptist Missionary Society was formed and he was sent to India where he preached, taught, and did Bible translation. After students at Williams College felt the call of God to join Carey (the so-called Haystack Prayer Meeting of 1806), the first American foreign sending society, the American Board of Commissioners for Foreign Missions, emerged in 1810. Adoniram Judson (1788–1850) was America's first missionary. Ordained a Congregationalist in New England, he joined Carey in 1812 under the American Board. After embracing Baptist views, his greatest labors were in Burma where he translated the Bible. Hudson Taylor (1832–1905) founded the China Inland Mission in 1865. His unflagging faith in God and passion to make Christ known became a model for independent missions around the world.

Chart 13

Charles Finney and Finneyism

Charles Finney:
Shaper of American Revivalism

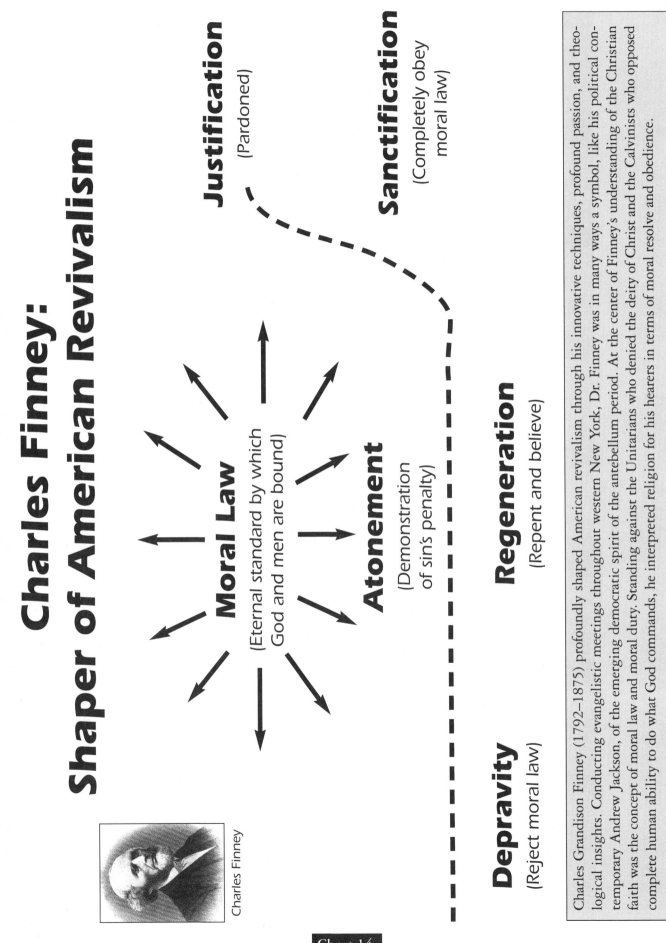

Charles Finney

Moral Law
(Eternal standard by which God and men are bound)

Atonement
(Demonstration of sin's penalty)

Justification
(Pardoned)

Sanctification
(Completely obey moral law)

Regeneration
(Repent and believe)

Depravity
(Reject moral law)

Charles Grandison Finney (1792–1875) profoundly shaped American revivalism through his innovative techniques, profound passion, and theological insights. Conducting evangelistic meetings throughout western New York, Dr. Finney was in many ways a symbol, like his political contemporary Andrew Jackson, of the emerging democratic spirit of the antebellum period. At the center of Finney's understanding of the Christian faith was the concept of moral law and moral duty. Standing against the Unitarians who denied the deity of Christ and the Calvinists who opposed complete human ability to do what God commands, he interpreted religion for his hearers in terms of moral resolve and obedience.

Chart 14

Charles Finney and the Death of Christ: A Legal Warning

The Grotian View of the Atonement
Governmental

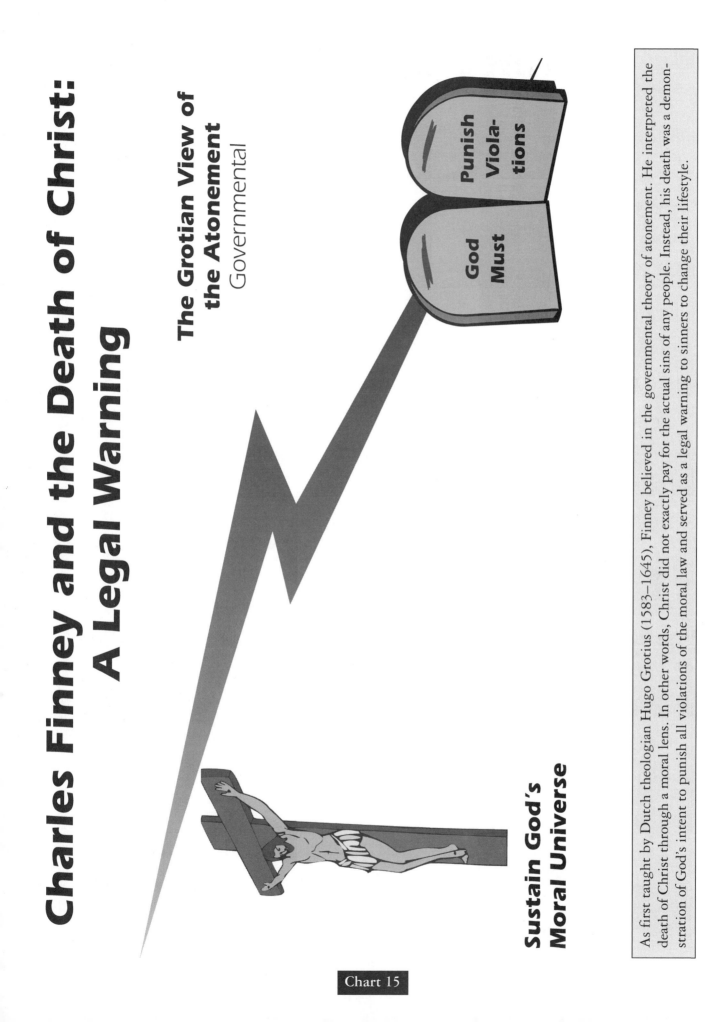

Punish Violations

God Must

Sustain God's Moral Universe

As first taught by Dutch theologian Hugo Grotius (1583–1645), Finney believed in the governmental theory of atonement. He interpreted the death of Christ through a moral lens. In other words, Christ did not exactly pay for the actual sins of any people. Instead, his death was a demonstration of God's intent to punish all violations of the moral law and served as a legal warning to sinners to change their lifestyle.

Chart 15

Finney and Salvation

The Sinner's Role

"No change is needed in God—neither in His character, in His government, nor in His position toward sinners. The utmost possible change and all the needed change is required on the part of the sinner. . . . God cannot afford to lose your influence in the universe. He will rejoice to use you for the glory of His mercy, if you will."

—The Salvation of Sinners Is Impossible

The Preacher's Task

"The great difficulty is to persuade sinners to choose right. God is ready to forgive them if they will repent; but the great problem is to persuade them to do so. . . . Here is the difficulty. Some have formed habits and have confirmed them until they have become immensely strong, and become exceedingly difficult to break."

—Salvation Is Difficult . . .

Finney believed that sinners had the ability to come to Christ, just a reluctance to do so. Finney also redefined the role of the preacher in gospel presentation. It was not merely the task of the preacher to present the claims of Christ, but to destroy moral resistance to Christ. Although Finney is to be admired for his zeal for souls, he denied original sin, substitutionary atonement, justification, and the need for regeneration by the Holy Spirit.

Chart 16

The Rise of Utopian Societies and the Classic American Cults

The Nineteenth Century: Rise of the Cults

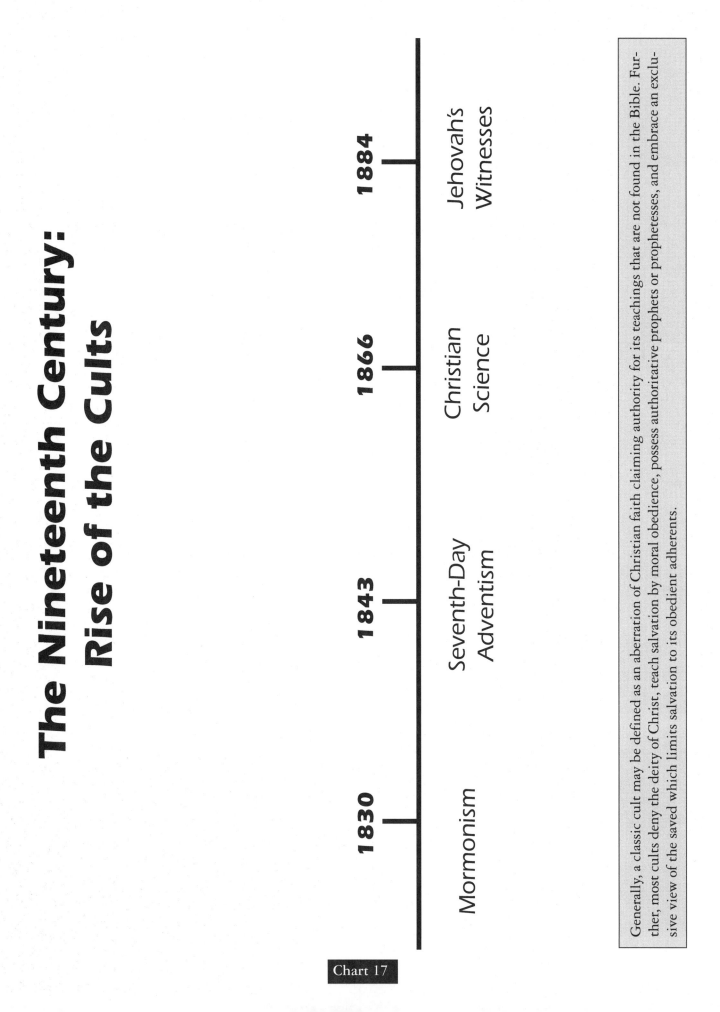

1830	1843	1866	1884
Mormonism	Seventh-Day Adventism	Christian Science	Jehovah's Witnesses

Generally, a classic cult may be defined as an aberration of Christian faith claiming authority for its teachings that are not found in the Bible. Further, most cults deny the deity of Christ, teach salvation by moral obedience, possess authoritative prophets or prophetesses, and embrace an exclusive view of the saved which limits salvation to its obedient adherents.

Chart 17

The Leaders and Shapers of Mormonism

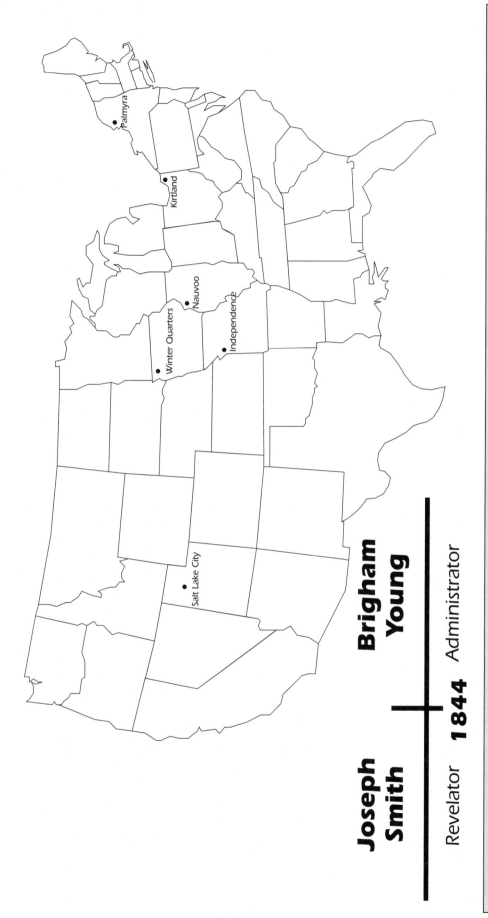

	Palmyra
Kirtland	
	Nauvoo
Winter Quarters	Independence
Salt Lake City	

Joseph Smith

Revelator **1844** Administrator

Brigham Young

Mormonism, the Church of Jesus Christ, Latter Day Saints, was established with the publication of *The Book of Mormon* in Palmyra, New York, in 1830. Joseph Smith (1805–44), who also wrote *The Doctrines and the Covenants* and *The Pearl of Great Price*, led his ever-increasing band of followers westward seeking religious freedom, first to Kirtland, Ohio, then Nauvoo, Illinois, then Independence, Missouri. After Smith's death in 1844, Mormons, under the direction of their new leader Brigham Young (1801–77), made a heroic trek across the Great Plains and settled in modern-day Utah.

Chart 18

The Theology of Mormonism

Authority　　Book of Mormon, revelations of apostles

God　　God was once a man, has body; polytheism—man becomes a god

Christ　　Divine but not unique

Atonement　　Erased effect of Adam's sin

Man　　Preexistent

Sin　　Innate goodness

Salvation　　By faith, baptism, laying on of hands, keeping commandments

Church　　No church from the apostle John to Joseph Smith (AD 95–1830); exclusivist

Eschatology　　Israel (American Indians) restored; millennial reign of Christ in Jerusalem (Independence, Missouri)

Judgment　　Second chance after death; all eventually advance to godhood

Practice　　No alcohol, tobacco, coffee, tea; fasting; tithing; Sabbath; baptism for dead

Mormonism teaches that salvation, human deification, is through works of righteousness. Christ, however, is not divine but a human being of amazing, though not unusual, attainments.

Chart 19

The Rise of the Seventh-Day Adventist Movement

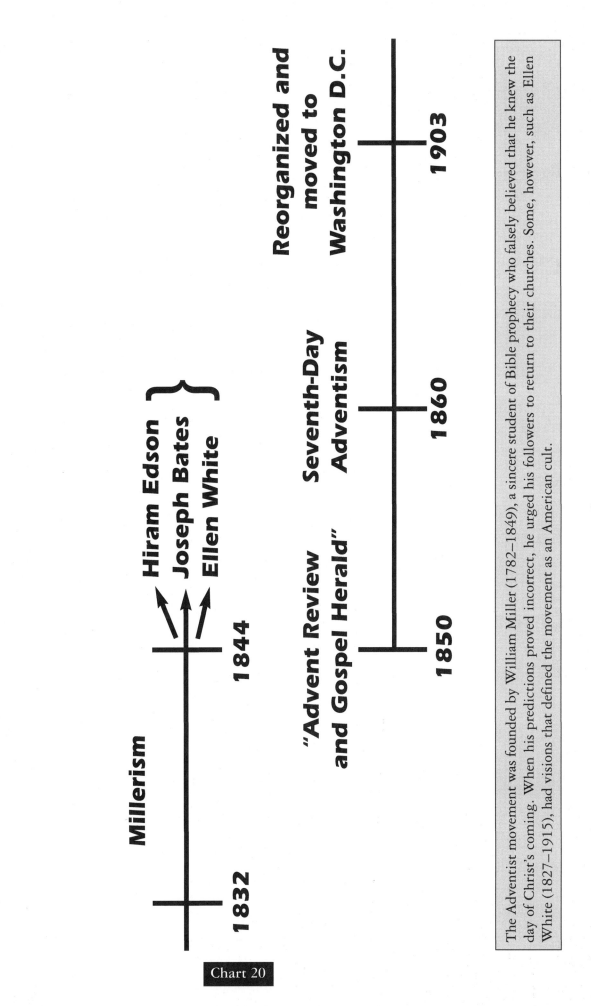

Millerism

1832

Hiram Edson
Joseph Bates
Ellen White

1844

"Advent Review and Gospel Herald"

Seventh-Day Adventism

Reorganized and moved to Washington D.C.

1850

1860

1903

Chart 20

The Adventist movement was founded by William Miller (1782–1849), a sincere student of Bible prophecy who falsely believed that he knew the day of Christ's coming. When his predictions proved incorrect, he urged his followers to return to their churches. Some, however, such as Ellen White (1827–1915), had visions that defined the movement as an American cult.

The Theology of Seventh-Day Adventism

Authority   Ellen G. White, continuing prophecies

God   Orthodox

Christ   Orthodox

Atonement   Substitutionary but incomplete

Man   Orthodox

Sin   Personal depravity

Salvation   By faith, obeying Mosaic law and Sabbath

Church   Exclusivist

Eschatology   Premillennial, post-tribulational

Judgment   Soul sleep, annihilation

Practice   OT dietary laws, Sabbath, believers' baptism, foot-washing

The Seventh-Day Adventist movement as expressed in Ellen White and others teaches that salvation is through Christ, though not completely so, because works must be added to it. Sunday worship is an evil practice.

Chart 21

The Theology of Christian Science

Authority	Mary Baker Eddy
God	Panentheism; matter does not exist
Christ	Divine idea; Jesus was a man
Atonement	Example
Man	Coeternal with God; bodies nonexistent
Sin	Imaginary
Salvation	Realization that sin does not exist
Church	Exclusivist; polity and doctrine cannot be changed without written permission from Mary Baker Eddy
Eschatology	None
Judgment	Probation to grow in truth; or annihilation
Practice	No sacraments

Mary Baker Eddy (1821–1910) established Christian Science based on her book, *Science and Health: A Key to Scripture*. Advocates deny the claims of Christ, believing that salvation is a present reality derived by mental confidence. Pain, like sin and death, does not exist; they are mental aberrations.

Chart 22

The Theology of Jehovah's Witnesses

Authority   Bible—New World Translation

God   Monotheism

Christ   Arian, unique, created

Atonement   Ransom, incomplete

Sin   Personal depravity (not total)

Salvation   Faith plus works

Church   Exclusivist

Eschatology   The 144,000 spend eternity in heaven, other Witnesses on earth

Judgment   Soul sleep and annihilation

Practice   No voting, holding office, saluting flag, taking oath, blood transfusions; pacifism

---

The Zion Watch Tower Society, Jehovah's Witness, was founded by Charles Taze Russell (1852–1916). Russell denied the essentials of Christian orthodoxy, teaching salvation by human endeavor.

Chart 23

The Antebellum and
Civil War Eras

The Presbyterian Schism of 1837: The New School and the Old School

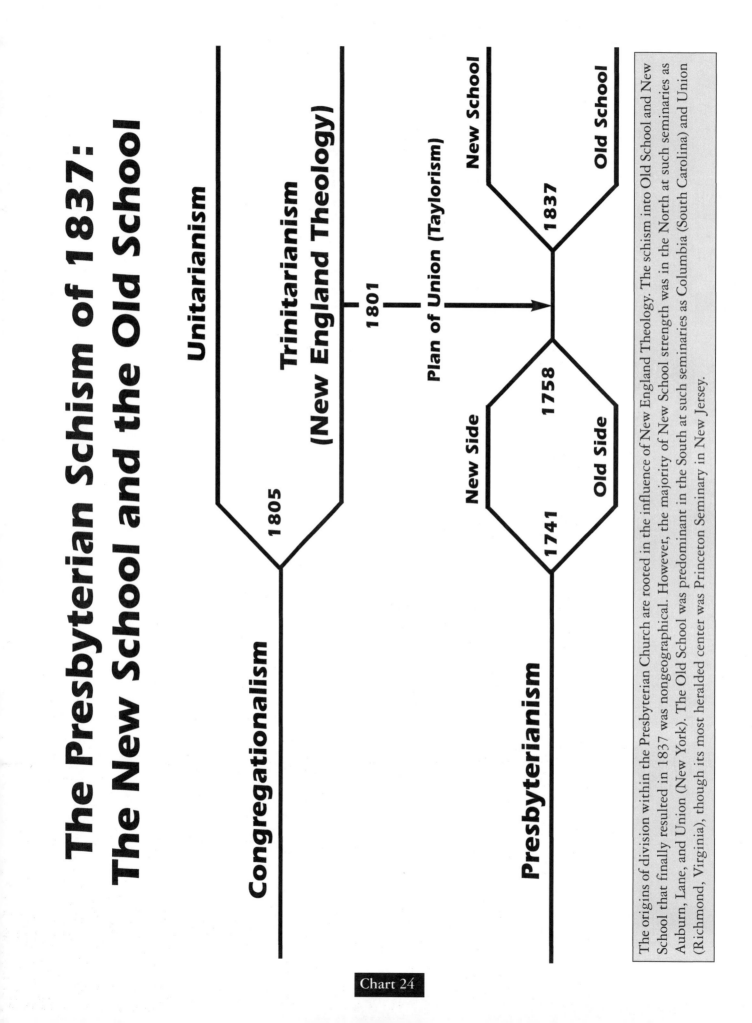

Unitarianism

Trinitarianism
(New England Theology)

1801

Plan of Union (Taylorism)

New School

Old School

1837

Congregationalism

1805

New Side

1758

Old Side

1741

Presbyterianism

The origins of division within the Presbyterian Church are rooted in the influence of New England Theology. The schism into Old School and New School that finally resulted in 1837 was nongeographical. However, the majority of New School strength was in the North at such seminaries as Auburn, Lane, and Union (New York). The Old School was predominant in the South at such seminaries as Columbia (South Carolina) and Union (Richmond, Virginia), though its most heralded center was Princeton Seminary in New Jersey.

Chart 24

The Influence of the Layman's Prayer Revival of 1858

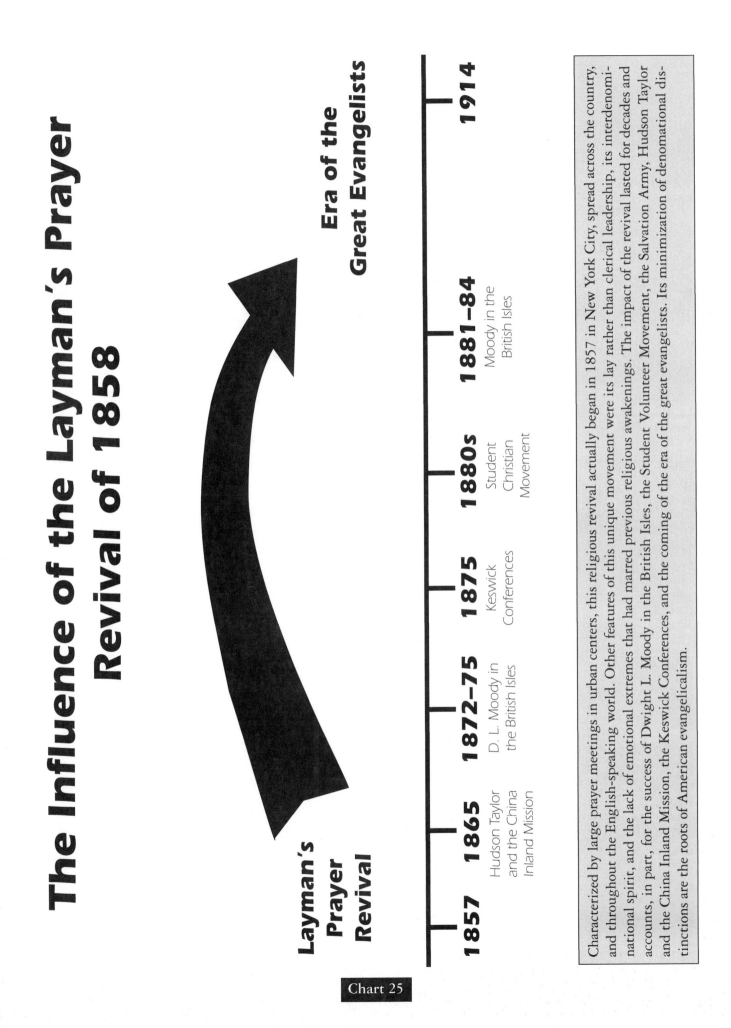

Layman's
Prayer
Revival

Era of the
Great Evangelists

1857	1865	1872–75	1875	1880s	1881–84	1914
	Hudson Taylor and the China Inland Mission	D. L. Moody in the British Isles	Keswick Conferences	Student Christian Movement	Moody in the British Isles	

Chart 25

Characterized by large prayer meetings in urban centers, this religious revival actually began in 1857 in New York City, spread across the country, and throughout the English-speaking world. Other features of this unique movement were its lay rather than clerical leadership, its interdenominational spirit, and the lack of emotional extremes that had marred previous religious awakenings. The impact of the revival lasted for decades and accounts, in part, for the success of Dwight L. Moody in the British Isles, the Student Volunteer Movement, the Salvation Army, Hudson Taylor and the China Inland Mission, the Keswick Conferences, and the coming of the era of the great evangelists. Its minimization of denominational distinctions are the roots of American evangelicalism.

National Contradiction: Equal but Inferior

The Irony of Thomas Jefferson

On Equality

"We hold these truths to be self evident: that all men are created equal; that they are endowed by their creator with certain inalienable rights; that among these are life, liberty, and the pursuit of happiness."

"[The king of Great Britain] has waged cruel war against human nature itself, violating its most sacred rights of life and liberty in the persons of a distant people who never offended him, captivating and carrying them into slavery."

—*Declaration of Independence*

On Inequality

"I advance it, therefore, as a suspicion only, that the blacks . . . are inferior to the whites in the endowments both of body and mind."

—*Notes on Virginia*

Jefferson maintained slaves throughout his life.

Thomas Jefferson manifested the contradictions of many of our national founders, equality for many yet a lesser status for some. Perhaps even more ironic, Abraham Lincoln, the Great Emancipator, advocated the notion of freeing the slaves, but not racial equality, once saying, "I am not nor ever have been in favor of bringing about in any way the social and political equality of the white and black races." Though the Union's victory in the Civil War officially ended slavery, it produced a freedom that still embraced racial prejudice.

Chart 26

Three American Revolutions: The Quest for Equality

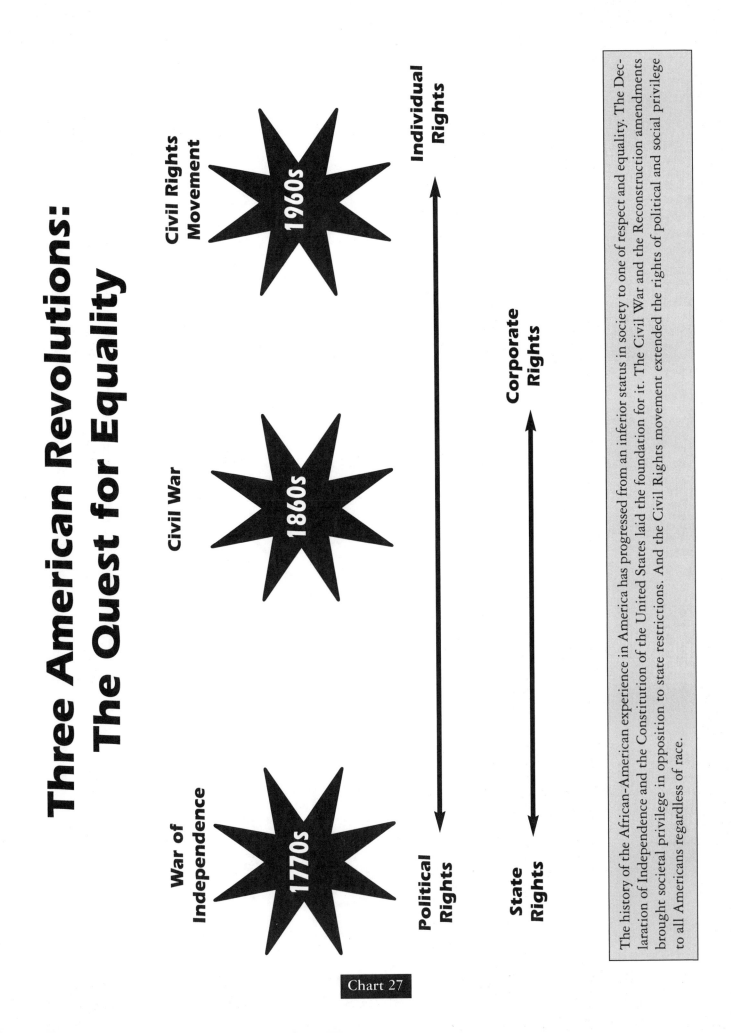

War of Independence

1770s

Civil War

1860s

Civil Rights Movement

1960s

Political Rights

Individual Rights

State Rights

Corporate Rights

The history of the African-American experience in America has progressed from an inferior status in society to one of respect and equality. The Declaration of Independence and the Constitution of the United States laid the foundation for it. The Civil War and the Reconstruction amendments brought societal privilege in opposition to state restrictions. And the Civil Rights movement extended the rights of political and social privilege to all Americans regardless of race.

Chart 27

The Baptists, Slavery, and Division

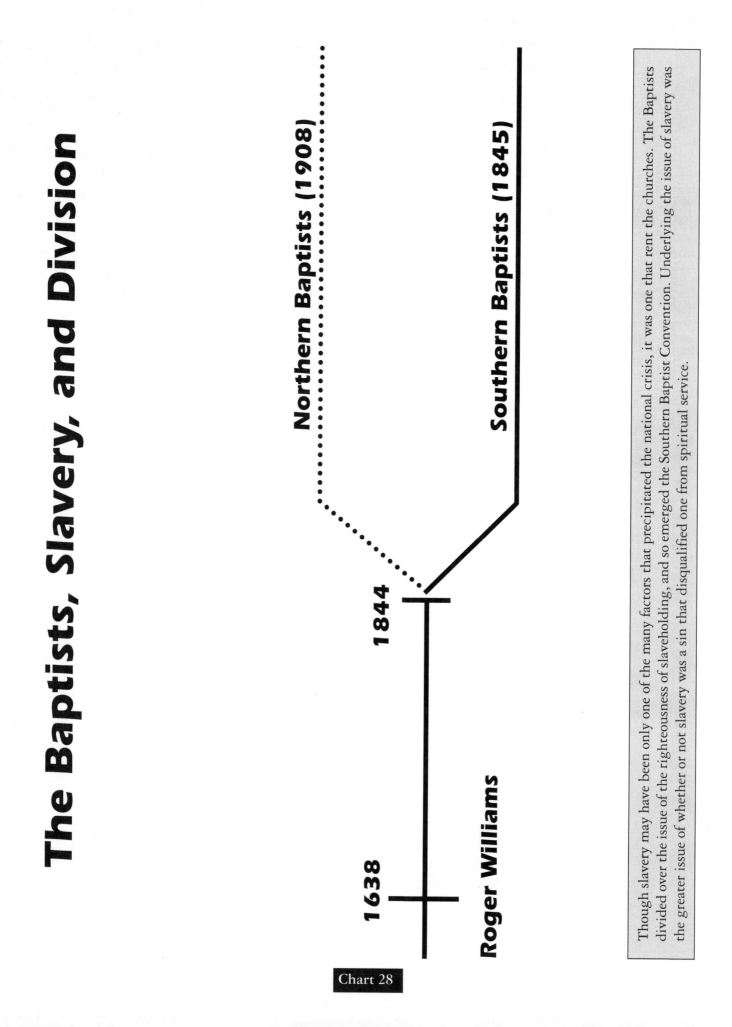

Northern Baptists (1908)

Southern Baptists (1845)

1844

1638

Roger Williams

Chart 28

Though slavery may have been only one of the many factors that precipitated the national crisis, it was one that rent the churches. The Baptists divided over the issue of the righteousness of slaveholding, and so emerged the Southern Baptist Convention. Underlying the issue of slavery was the greater issue of whether or not slavery was a sin that disqualified one from spiritual service.

The Presbyterians, Slavery, and Division

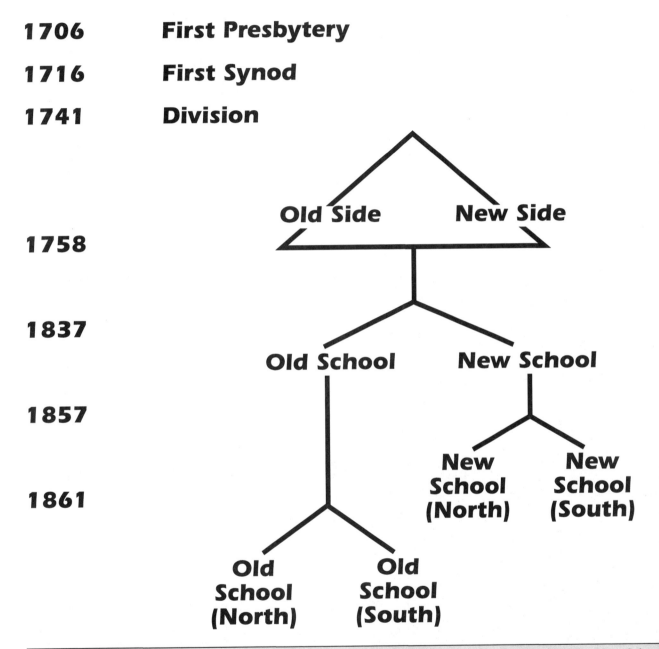

1706   **First Presbytery**

1716   **First Synod**

1741   **Division**

1758   Old Side   New Side

1837   Old School   New School

1857   New School (North)   New School (South)

1861   Old School (North)   Old School (South)

The Presbyterians came to the Civil War divided nonsectionally by the schism of 1837–38. The New School, perhaps more sensitive to social issues, divided in 1857, creating two sectional New School churches. Old Schoolers, who saw the crisis in more political terms, divided into two churches with the withdrawal of the Southern states from the Union. During the war, the New and Old Schools in the South merged to become the Presbyterian Church of the Confederate States of America, later renamed the Presbyterian Church in the United States. The Northern schools merged in 1869 to become the Presbyterian Church in the United States of America.

Chart 29

The Methodists, Slavery, and Division

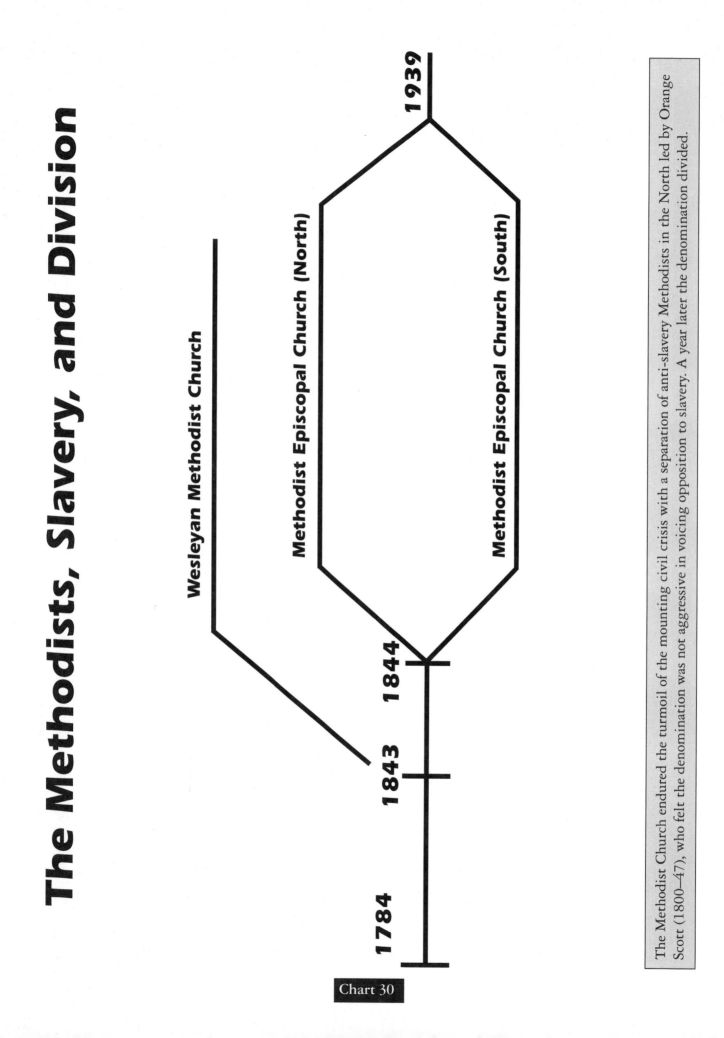

Wesleyan Methodist Church

Methodist Episcopal Church (North)

Methodist Episcopal Church (South)

1784

1843

1844

1939

Chart 30

The Methodist Church endured the turmoil of the mounting civil crisis with a separation of anti-slavery Methodists in the North led by Orange Scott (1800–47), who felt the denomination was not aggressive in voicing opposition to slavery. A year later the denomination divided.

THE MODERN PERIOD OF AMERICAN CHURCH HISTORY

The Background:
The Rise of Nineteenth-Century
European Liberalism

The Rise of the Sciences:

The Root of Change in Religious Understanding

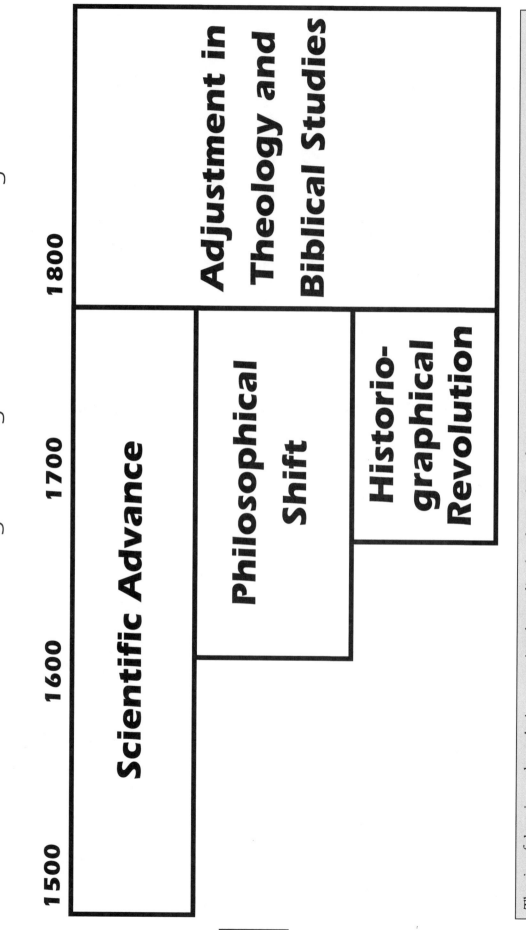

1500	1600	1700	1800

Scientific Advance

Philosophical Shift

Historio-graphical Revolution

Adjustment in Theology and Biblical Studies

The rise of the sciences brought into question the medieval understanding of the authority of the church and the interpretation of Scripture. Scientific advances seemed to push God out of the universe as supernatural causes were replaced by natural explanations and knowledge became restricted to the realm of the mental and physical. As a result, many felt that traditional views of Christian faith and the Bible were no longer viable.

Chart 31

The Biblical Support for the Medieval, Static Theory of the Universe

1. The Immobility of the Earth

Psalm 93:1; 96:10 "it cannot be moved"
Psalm 104:5 "earth . . . it can never be moved"
Ecclesiastes 1:4 "the earth remains forever"

2. The Mobility of the Sun

Joshua 10:12–13 "sun, stand still . . . so the sun stood still"
Psalm 104:19 "the sun knows when to go down"
Psalm 104:22 "the sun rises"

3. The Flatness of the Earth

Exodus 20:4
Deuteronomy 4:39; 5:8
1 Kings 8:23
Jeremiah 31:37

} "heavens above . . . earth beneath"

Medieval theologians believed that the Bible taught the immobility of the earth, the mobility of the sun, and the flatness of the earth. Even Martin Luther, the great Reformer, agreed and, along with his Roman Catholic opponents, condemned Copernicus's solar-centric astronomical theory. But did the new scientific discoveries really disprove the Bible or one theory about science falsely supported with biblical texts?

Chart 32

Hegel and the History of Civilization

Key to Change: The Geist (Spirit)

Motive of Change: Quest for self-consciousness

Process of Change: Nationalistic / Historicist

Method of Change: Dialecticalism (harmonization of opposites)

Oriental despotism vs. freedom = Greek world

Greek world vs. freedom = Roman world

Roman despotism vs. freedom = Christianity

Christianity vs. freedom = Secularism

(Industrial Age)

Chart 33

New views of approaching the Bible could not have been possible without new ways of looking at history, such as those proposed by Georg Hegel (1770–1831), the German idealist philosopher. Static views of the Bible, he said, are rooted in static views of history. A progressive understanding of the past allows for a progressive view of God's truth.

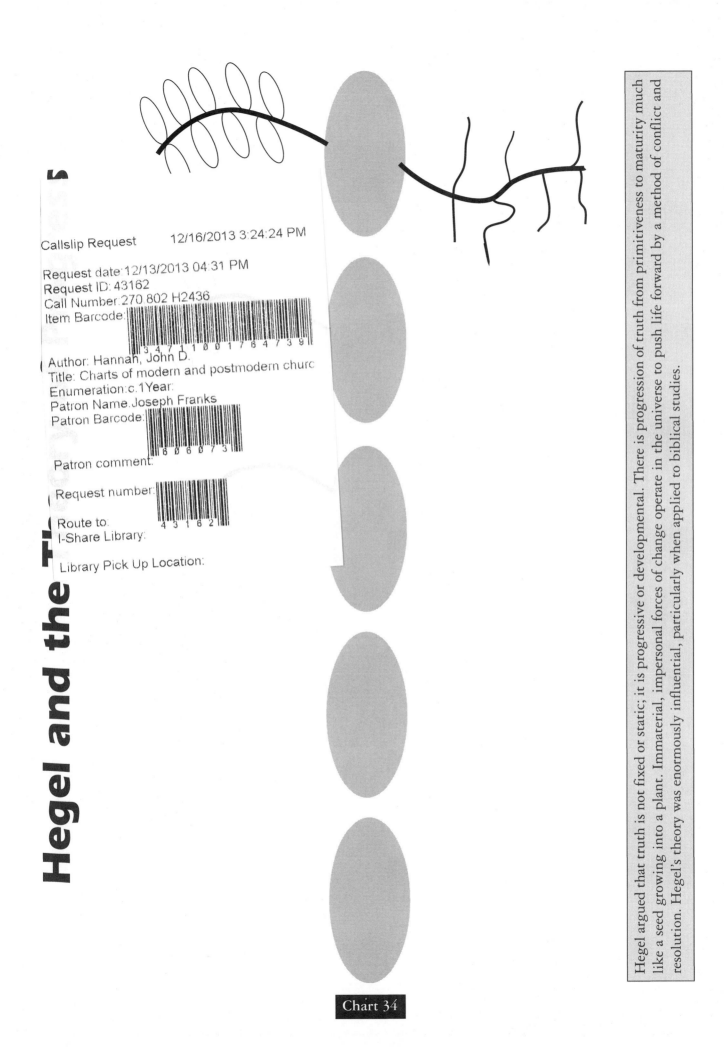

Hegel and the Th...

Hegel argued that truth is not fixed or static; it is progressive or developmental. There is progression of truth from primitiveness to maturity much like a seed growing into a plant. Immaterial, impersonal forces of change operate in the universe to push life forward by a method of conflict and resolution. Hegel's theory was enormously influential, particularly when applied to biblical studies.

Chart 34

Auguste Comte:
An Example of Progressive Thought

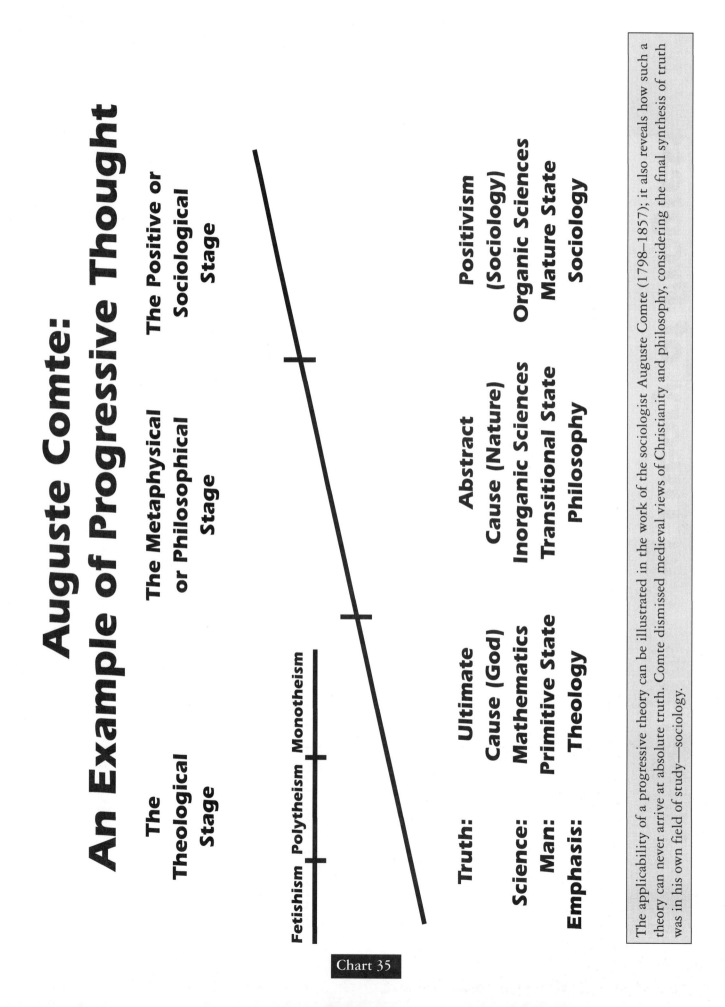

	The Theological Stage	The Metaphysical or Philosophical Stage	The Positive or Sociological Stage
	Fetishism Polytheism Monotheism		
Truth:	Ultimate Cause (God)	Abstract Cause (Nature)	Positivism (Sociology)
Science:	Mathematics	Inorganic Sciences	Organic Sciences
Man:	Primitive State	Transitional State	Mature State
Emphasis:	Theology	Philosophy	Sociology

Chart 35

The applicability of a progressive theory can be illustrated in the work of the sociologist Auguste Comte (1798–1857); it also reveals how such a theory can never arrive at absolute truth. Comte dismissed medieval views of Christianity and philosophy, considering the final synthesis of truth was in his own field of study—sociology.

The Enlightenment and Traditional Religion:

Schleiermacher's Attempt to Preserve True Religion

Chart 36

	Traditional Religion	SCHLEIERMACHER	Enlightenment
Focus of Religion	Revelation	Feeling	Reason
Revelation	From Without (God Speaking)	From Within (Man Emotionally Perceiving/Feeling)	From Within (Man Reasoning)
Christ	Divine/Human Revealer	Human Archetype of God Consciousness	Human Archetype of Morality

Faced with a religious crisis initiated by scientific, philosophical, and literary advances, Christianity's defenders responded in different ways. Friedrich Schleiermacher (1768–1834) is recognized as "Father of Nineteenth-Century Liberalism" for his methodological approach. Schleiermacher rejected the Enlightenment philosophers who rooted authority in human rationality, but felt that traditional concepts of the Bible's authority would not preserve the faith from rational criticism. He, therefore, placed religion in the realm of emotional experience, that unfalsifiable fortress of personal witness. The fruit of his attempt to restructure Christianity on this basis was a Bible that only verified experience and a Christ who was the best human example of subjective piety.

Albrecht Ritschl:

Liberalism and the Reduction of Christianity to Ethics

"Christianity, then, is the monotheistic, completely spiritual, and ethical religion, which, based on the life of its Author as Redeemer and as Founder of the Kingdom of God, consists in the freedom of children of God, involves the impulse to conduct from the motive of love, aims at the moral organization of mankind, and grounds blessedness on the relation of sonship to God, as well as on the Kingdom of God."

"Christianity . . . resembles not a circle described from a single center, but an ellipse which is determined by two foci."

—The Christian Doctrine of Justification and Reconciliation

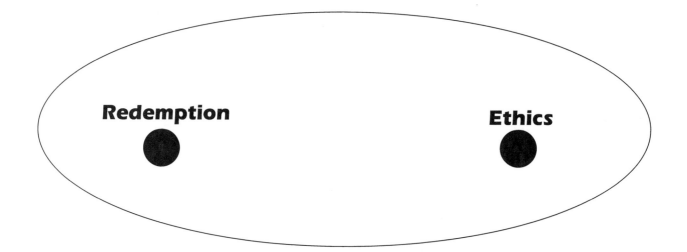

Albrecht Ritschl (1822–89) attempted to establish Christian faith on a more objective basis than Schleiermacher. So doing, he placed the Christian doctrine of salvation (as well as the rest of theology) in the realm of ethics. Christianity was defensible for him because it was more than subjective expression, but it was not scientific. It was an expression of morals.

Chart 37

Liberalism and the History of Religions School

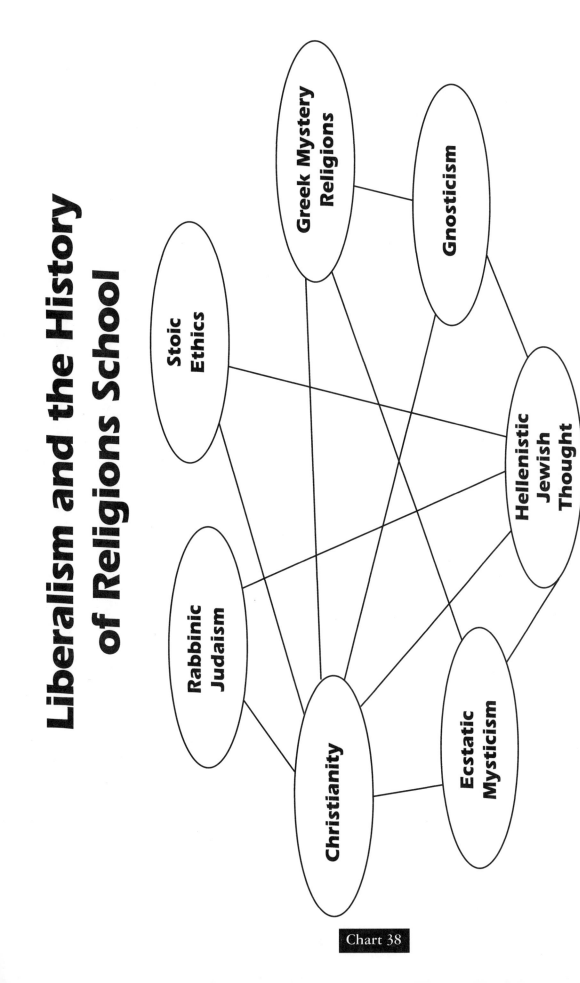

Greek Mystery Religions

Stoic Ethics

Gnosticism

Rabbinic Judaism

Hellenistic Jewish Thought

Christianity

Ecstatic Mysticism

Chart 38

A group of German scholars emerged between 1880 and 1920 who sought to discover the essence of Christian faith in the study of comparative religions. True religion was found in what all religions share in common. While Jesus was viewed as a historical figure, details were lacking to really understand him as other than a human being whom Paul, influenced by the pagan mystery religions and Gnosticism, had horribly disfigured.

The Pioneers of the Theory of Evolution

Erasmus Darwin (Charles' grandfather)
(1731–1802)

Jean Baptiste de Lamarck
(1744–1829)

Sir Charles Lyell
(1797–1875)

Charles Darwin
(1809–82)

**Charles Darwin
(1809–82)**

Author of *Origin of the Species* (1859) and *Descent of Man* (1871), Charles Darwin has been one of our culture's most influential figures since the nineteenth century. Though he alone did not pioneer the concept of biological evolution, his research raised it to scientific status and popularity never achieved by his predecessors. In effect, his speculations appeared to many to prove that design was possible in the universe without a designer, thereby destroying a much-used argument for the existence of God.

Chart 39

The Rise of American
Liberalism, the "New Theology"

Protestantism in Nineteenth-Century England

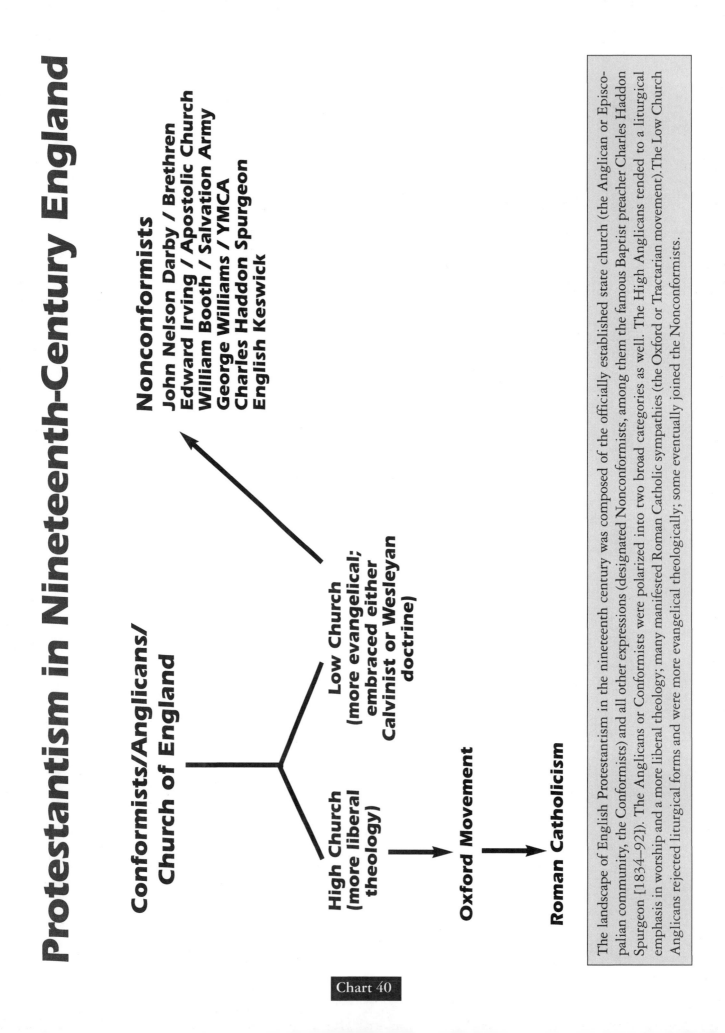

Nonconformists
John Nelson Darby / Brethren
Edward Irving / Apostolic Church
William Booth / Salvation Army
George Williams / YMCA
Charles Haddon Spurgeon
English Keswick

Conformists/Anglicans/
Church of England

Low Church
(more evangelical;
embraced either
Calvinist or Wesleyan
doctrine)

High Church
(more liberal
theology)

Oxford Movement

Roman Catholicism

Chart 40

The landscape of English Protestantism in the nineteenth century was composed of the officially established state church (the Anglican or Episcopalian community, the Conformists) and all other expressions (designated Nonconformists, among them the famous Baptist preacher Charles Haddon Spurgeon [1834–92]). The Anglicans or Conformists were polarized into two broad categories as well. The High Anglicans tended to a liturgical emphasis in worship and a more liberal theology; many manifested Roman Catholic sympathies (the Oxford or Tractarian movement). The Low Church Anglicans rejected liturgical forms and were more evangelical theologically; some eventually joined the Nonconformists.

The Historical Sources of

Nineteenth-Century American Liberalism

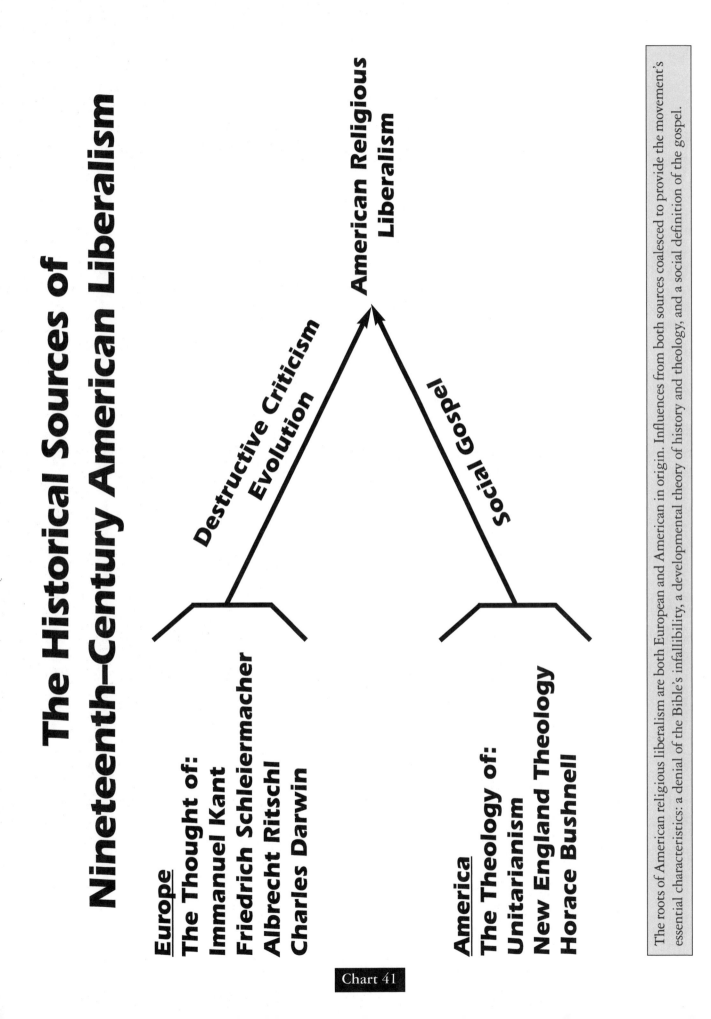

Europe
The Thought of:
Immanuel Kant
Friedrich Schleiermacher
Albrecht Ritschl
Charles Darwin

Destructive Criticism
Evolution

American Religious
Liberalism

Social Gospel

America
The Theology of:
Unitarianism
New England Theology
Horace Bushnell

Chart 41

The roots of American religious liberalism are both European and American in origin. Influences from both sources coalesced to provide the movement's essential characteristics: a denial of the Bible's infallibility, a developmental theory of history and theology, and a social definition of the gospel.

The Assumptions of "New Theology"

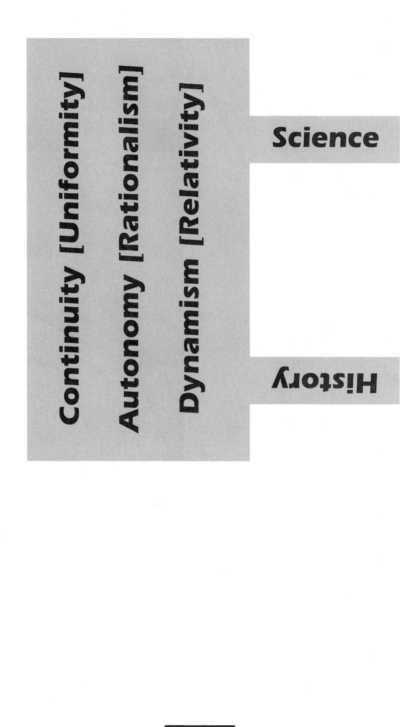

Continuity [Uniformity]

Autonomy [Rationalism]

Dynamism [Relativity]

Science

History

Liberalism was designated by it advocates as the "New Theology." Embracing the "authoritative" findings of the sciences, proponents called for a revision of Christianity. The movement had three central beliefs: a progressive rather than a catastrophic view of history, the authority of reason, and relativity. The emphasis on reason made the movement an heir of the Enlightenment; the notion of relativity was its ultimate undoing.

Chart 42

The "New Theology" and the Bible

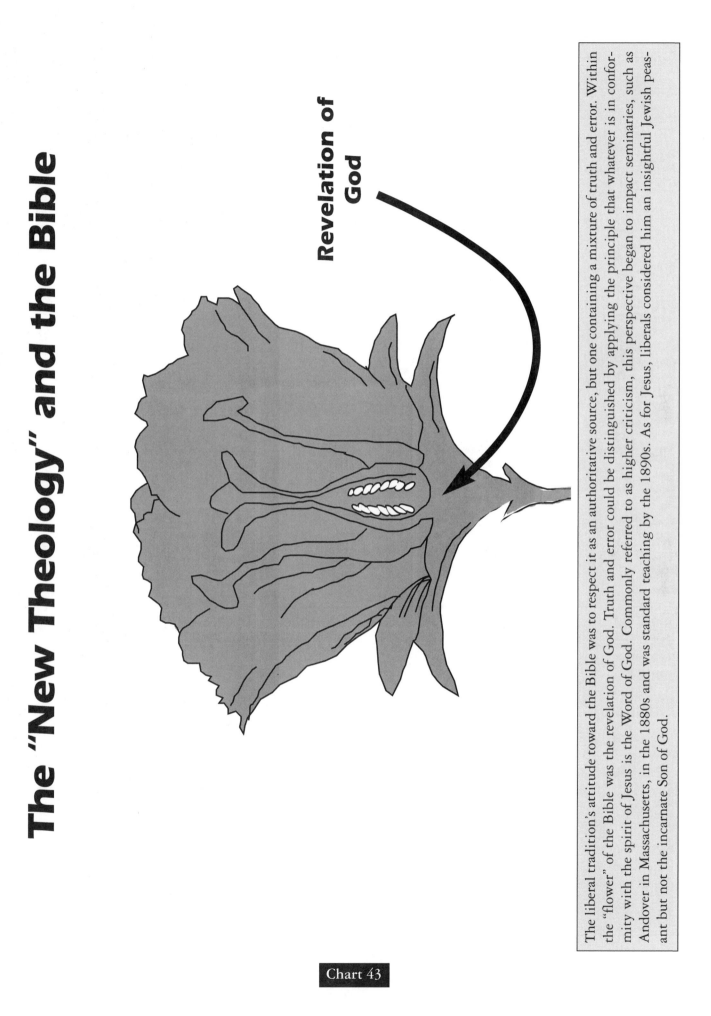

Revelation of God

The liberal tradition's attitude toward the Bible was to respect it as an authoritative source, but one containing a mixture of truth and error. Within the "flower" of the Bible was the revelation of God. Truth and error could be distinguished by applying the principle that whatever is in conformity with the spirit of Jesus is the Word of God. Commonly referred to as higher criticism, this perspective began to impact seminaries, such as Andover in Massachusetts, in the 1880s and was standard teaching by the 1890s. As for Jesus, liberals considered him an insightful Jewish peasant but not the incarnate Son of God.

Chart 43

The History of the American Liberal Tradition

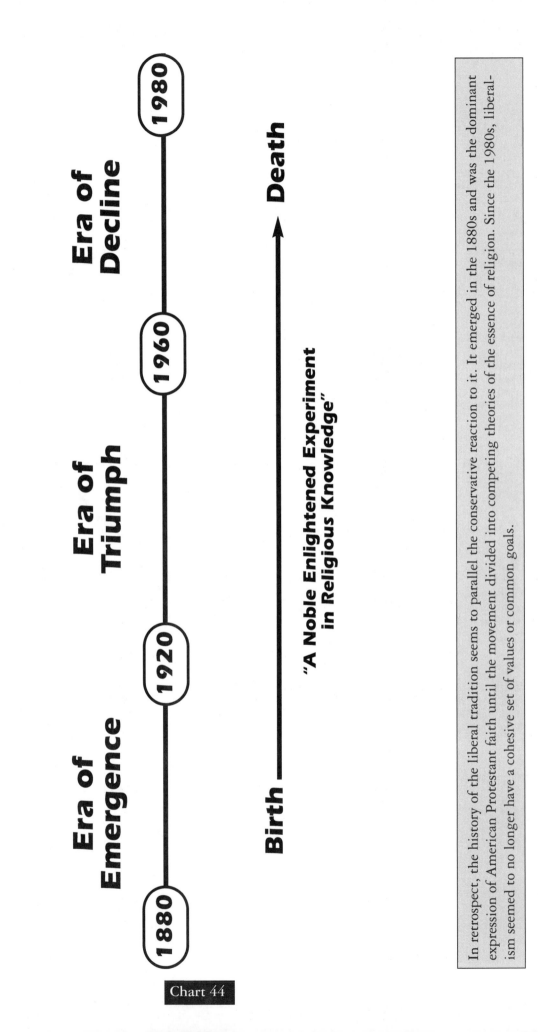

Era of Emergence

Era of Triumph

Era of Decline

1880 — 1920 — 1960 — 1980

Birth ──────────→ Death

"A Noble Enlightened Experiment in Religious Knowledge"

Chart 44

In retrospect, the history of the liberal tradition seems to parallel the conservative reaction to it. It emerged in the 1880s and was the dominant expression of American Protestant faith until the movement divided into competing theories of the essence of religion. Since the 1980s, liberalism seemed to no longer have a cohesive set of values or common goals.

Liberal Theology and Evangelical Theology: A Comparison

	Liberal Theology	Evangelical Theology
Authority	Individual experience	God's character and Word
God	Immanent only, all love, no wrath	Personal, holy, infinite
Supernatural	No miracles, natural and supernatural same	Supernatural since God transcends nature
Christ	A good man, ethical teacher, an example	Completely God and man, born of a virgin
Man	Innate goodness, divinity within	Totally depraved, in God's image
Sin	Evil a remnant of animal instincts	Fallen and guilty
Salvation	Conversion an acknowledgment of deity within man	Instanteous salvation from sin
Future	No hell, fulfillment now	Eternal life or death
Church	Concerned with saving world and society	Concerned with the salvation of souls

J. Gresham Machen (1881–1937), the conservative Presbyterian stalwart of the 1920s, argued in *Christianity and Liberalism* (1923) that liberalism was not simply an aberrant form of Christianity; it was not Christianity at all. In fact, he perceived it as an intellectually retrograde movement because it failed to be informed by all available knowledge.

Chart 45

Denominational Strife and the Rise of Evangelicalism (1880–1930)

The History of American Evangelicalism

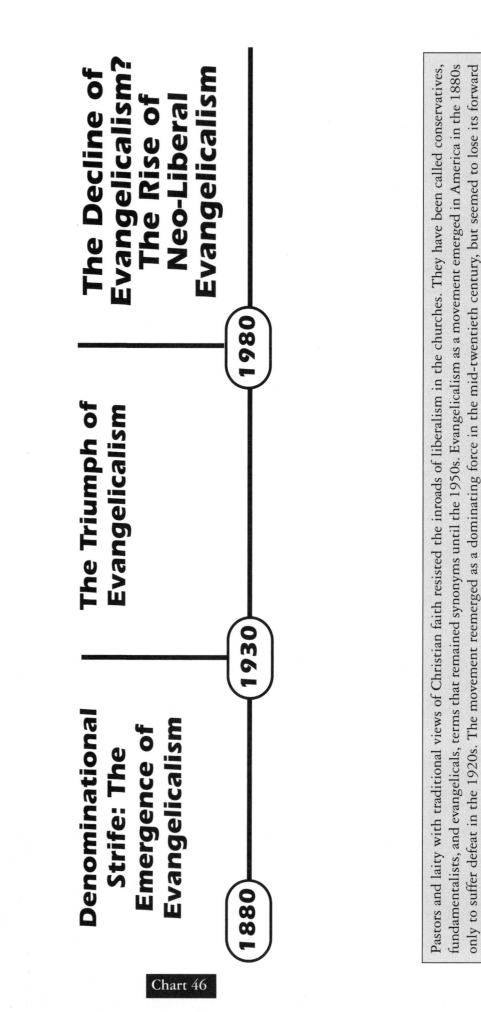

Denominational Strife: The Emergence of Evangelicalism

The Triumph of Evangelicalism

The Decline of Evangelicalism? The Rise of Neo-Liberal Evangelicalism

1880

1930

1980

Chart 46

Pastors and laity with traditional views of Christian faith resisted the inroads of liberalism in the churches. They have been called conservatives, fundamentalists, and evangelicals, terms that remained synonyms until the 1950s. Evangelicalism as a movement emerged in America in the 1880s only to suffer defeat in the 1920s. The movement reemerged as a dominating force in the mid-twentieth century, but seemed to lose its forward momentum when it fractured into competing emphases in the 1980s.

The Origin of the Bible Institutes in America

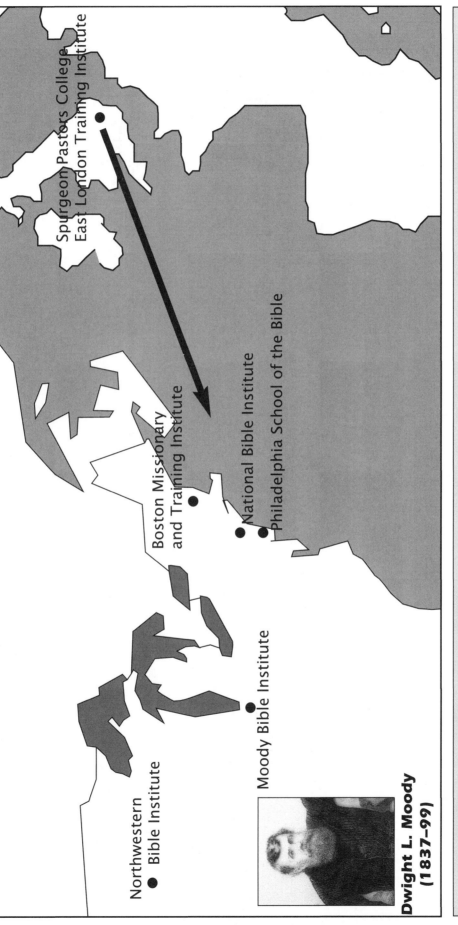

Spurgeon Pastors College
East London Training Institute

National Bible Institute

Philadelphia School of the Bible

Boston Missionary
and Training Institute

Northwestern
Bible Institute

Moody Bible Institute

**Dwight L. Moody
(1837–99)**

One of the early reactions to liberal religious trends in education was the emergence of Bible institutes and later Bible colleges. Their original intent was to prepare an army of church workers and missionaries. Only later did they purpose to train pastors for the churches. One of those schools, Moody Bible Institute in Chicago, was named for the most famous evangelist of the late nineteenth century, Dwight Lyman Moody (1837–99). Moody emerged from poverty to prominence with an ability to appeal to the masses in America and England; he preached a message of ruin through sin and redemption through Christ.

Chart 47

The Northern Baptists and the Fundamentalist Movement

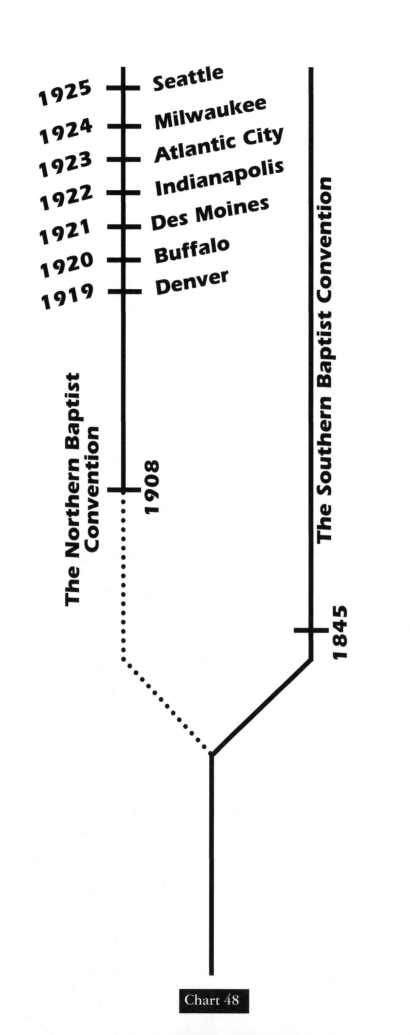

1925 — Seattle
1924 — Milwaukee
1923 — Atlantic City
1922 — Indianapolis
1921 — Des Moines
1920 — Buffalo
1919 — Denver

The Northern Baptist Convention

1908

The Southern Baptist Convention

1845

Chart 48

Though Baptists in America divided in the Civil War era, northern Baptists did not form a fellowship as immediately as did their southern counterparts. When the convention did form, the impetus was largely from liberal perspectives, causing controversy in the 1920s. Conservatives in the convention struggled at their annual gatherings to maintain a narrow theology, obtain a binding creed, investigate the seminaries, and deal with liberal inroads in the missions program. They did not succeed.

The Course of Theological Development within Northern Presbyterianism

Old School	New School

Merger
1869

Revision Attempted
1889

Westminster Confession Altered
1903

Auburn Affirmation
1924

New Confession
1967

THEOLOGICAL MERGER

THEOLOGICAL REVISION

One example of the conservative-liberal struggle can be seen in the Presbyterian denomination. Following the reunion of New School and Old School factions after the Civil War to form the Presbyterian Church in the United States of America, powerful liberal spokesmen called for revision of the church's doctrinal standards, finally resulting in the alteration of the Westminster Confession. Later, the Auburn Affirmation called for a wider perspective on traditional orthodoxy and the New Confession allowed for it.

Chart 49

Northern Presbyterians and the Conflict at Princeton

1902   Seminary Administratively Separated from University

1909   The Student Revolt

1913   A New President

THEOLOGICAL DISCORD

1920   Plan of Union of Evangelical Churches

1921   Death of B. B. Warfield

1922   Harry Emerson Fosdick Case

1923   Auburn Affirmation

1924   Charles Erdman's Election as Moderator

1926   Investigation of Discord

1929   Reorganization

For many conservative Presbyterians, the death knell sounded when Princeton Seminary reorganized in 1929 and broadened its theological stance at the same time. Troubles had been brewing for over a decade before the reorganization, but the actual event precipitated J. Gresham Machen's resignation from the faculty.

Chart 50

The Northern Presbyterians
and the Missions Controversy

1921	1932	1933	1935
Thomas's Report on China	Rethinking Missions	Independent Board of Foreign Missions	Machen Defrocked

Chart 51

The Presbyterian Church also was rocked by controversy over missions. After W. H. Griffith Thomas (1861–1924), a retired Anglican scholar living in Philadelphia, reported of liberal influence in China, J. Gresham Machen established an independent foreign missions board in 1933. The action contributed to Machen's dismissal from the denomination in 1935. The next year he was among the founders of the Orthodox Presbyterian Church.

Evangelicalism's Triumph, Evangelicalism Today (1930–Present)

The Realignment of Evangelicalism in the 1930s and 1940s

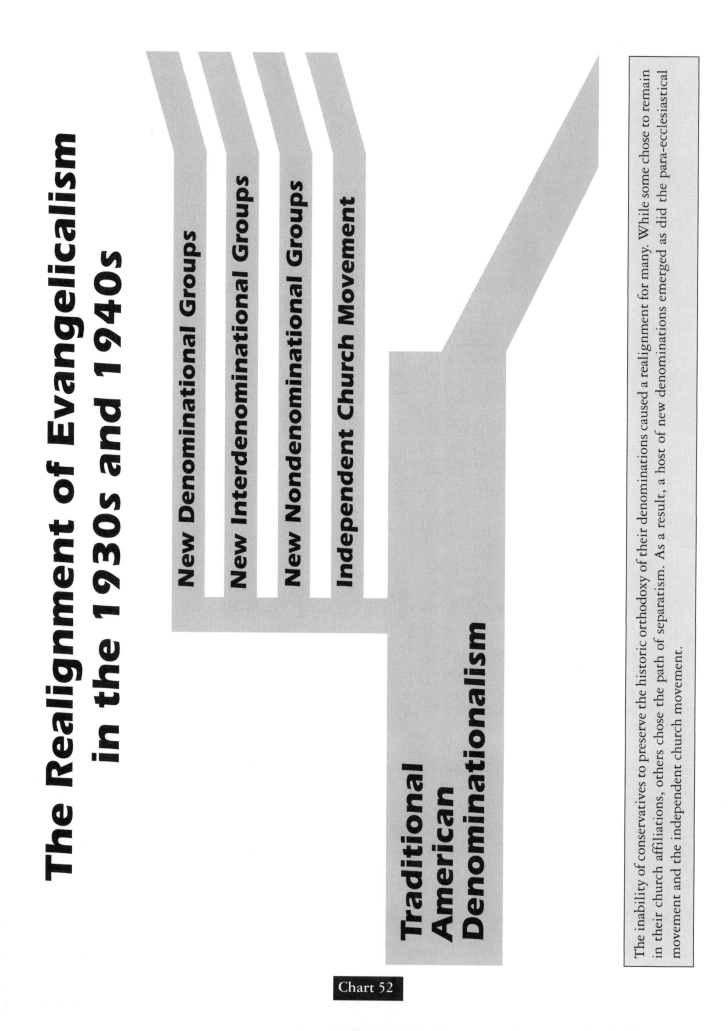

New Denominational Groups

New Interdenominational Groups

New Nondenominational Groups

Independent Church Movement

Traditional American Denominationalism

Chart 52

The inability of conservatives to preserve the historic orthodoxy of their denominations caused a realignment for many. While some chose to remain in their church affiliations, others chose the path of separatism. As a result, a host of new denominations emerged as did the para-ecclesiastical movement and the independent church movement.

The Restructuring of Evangelicalism:

The Building of a New Coalition

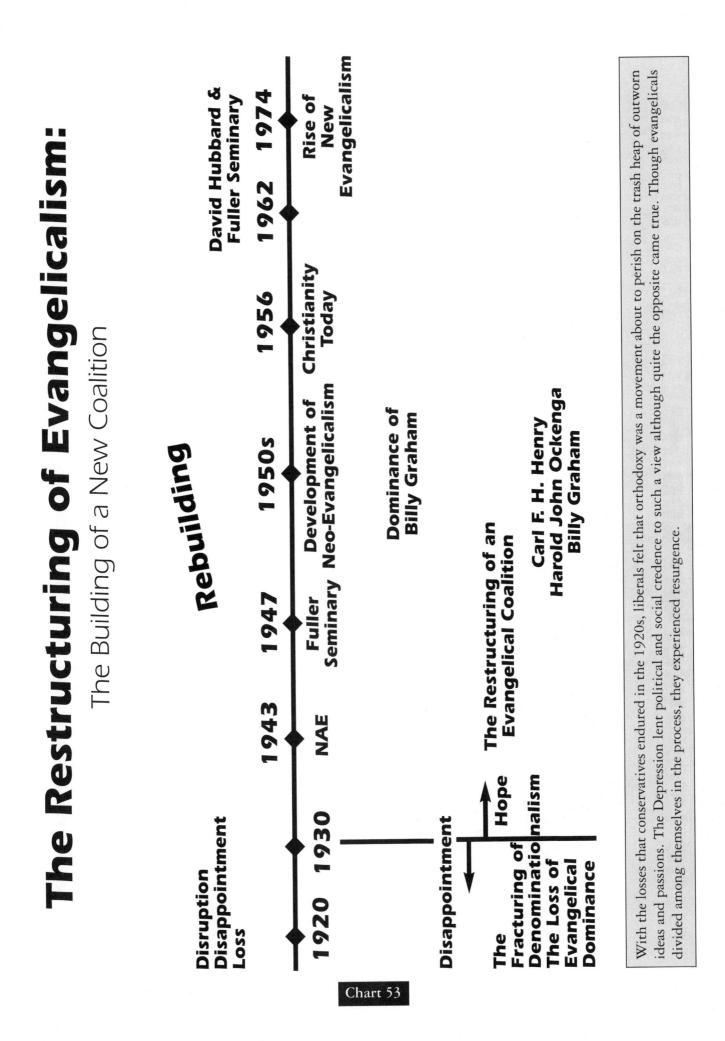

Rebuilding

Disruption
Disappointment
Loss

| 1920 | 1930 | 1943 | 1947 | 1950s | 1956 | 1962 | 1974 |

NAE

Fuller
Seminary

Development of
Neo-Evangelicalism

Christianity
Today

David Hubbard &
Fuller Seminary

Rise of
New
Evangelicalism

Dominance of
Billy Graham

The Restructuring of an
Evangelical Coalition

Carl F. H. Henry
Harold John Ockenga
Billy Graham

Disappointment

Hope

The
Fracturing of
Denominationalism
The Loss of
Evangelical
Dominance

Chart 53

With the losses that conservatives endured in the 1920s, liberals felt that orthodoxy was a movement about to perish on the trash heap of outworn ideas and passions. The Depression lent political and social credence to such a view although quite the opposite came true. Though evangelicals divided among themselves in the process, they experienced resurgence.

The Presbyterian Separatist Movement

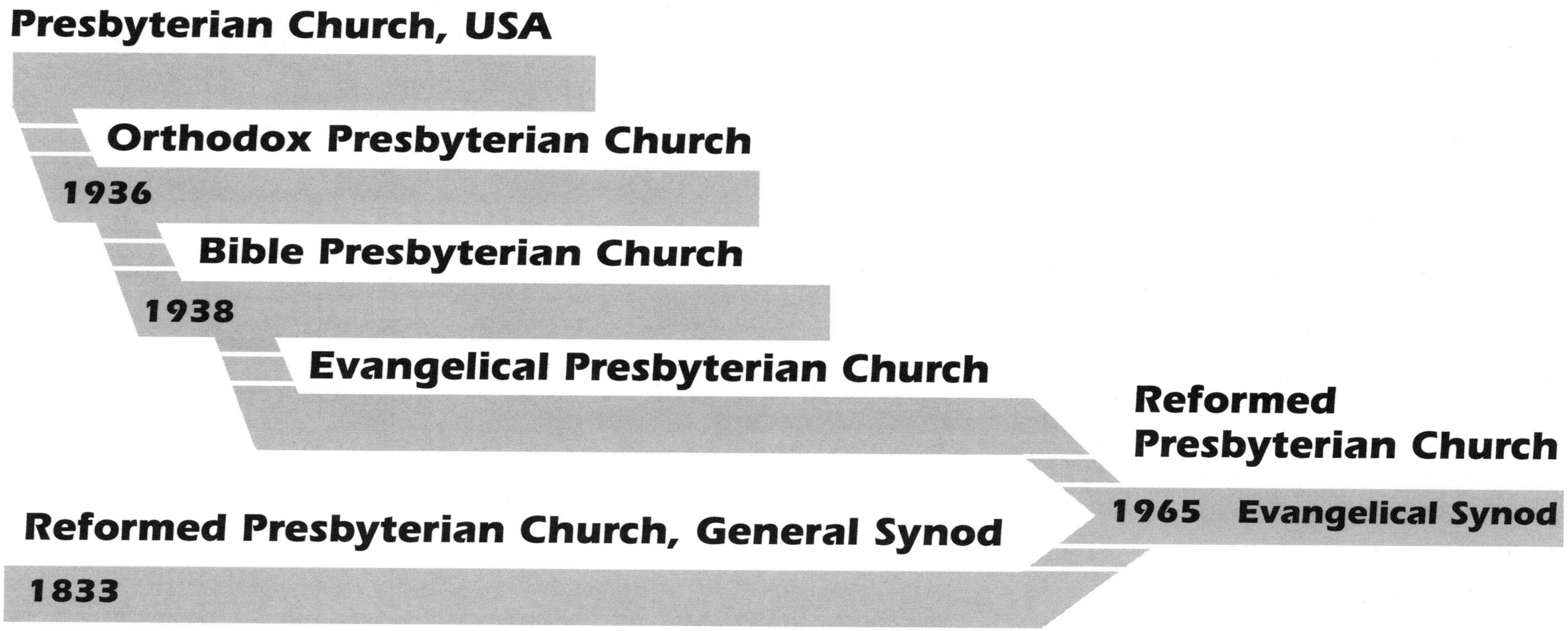

Presbyterian Church, USA

Orthodox Presbyterian Church

1936

Bible Presbyterian Church

1938

Evangelical Presbyterian Church

Reformed
Presbyterian Church

1965 Evangelical Synod

Reformed Presbyterian Church, General Synod

1833

Chart 54

The inability of conservative Presbyterians to maintain creedal orthodoxy in their denomination led to separation beginning in the 1930s. Unfortunately, the history of the movement has been one of intramural controversy and further divisions.

The Northern Baptist Separatist Movement

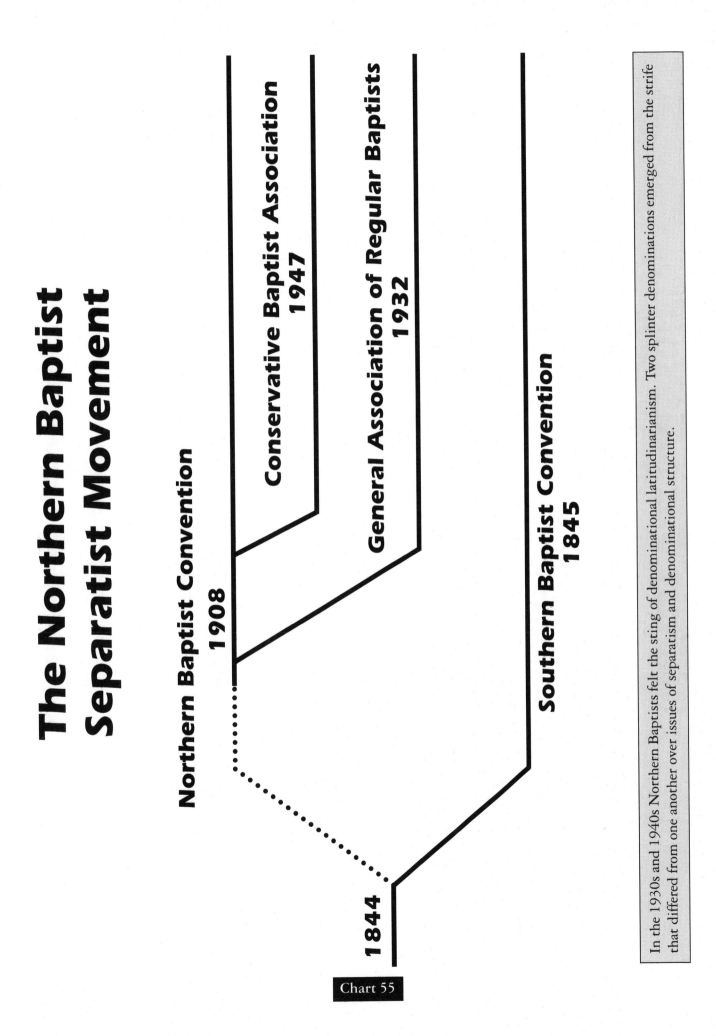

Northern Baptist Convention 1908

Conservative Baptist Association 1947

General Association of Regular Baptists 1932

Southern Baptist Convention 1845

1844

Chart 55

In the 1930s and 1940s Northern Baptists felt the sting of denominational latitudinarianism. Two splinter denominations emerged from the strife that differed from one another over issues of separatism and denominational structure.

Baptist Separatism:
The Baptist Bible Fellowship

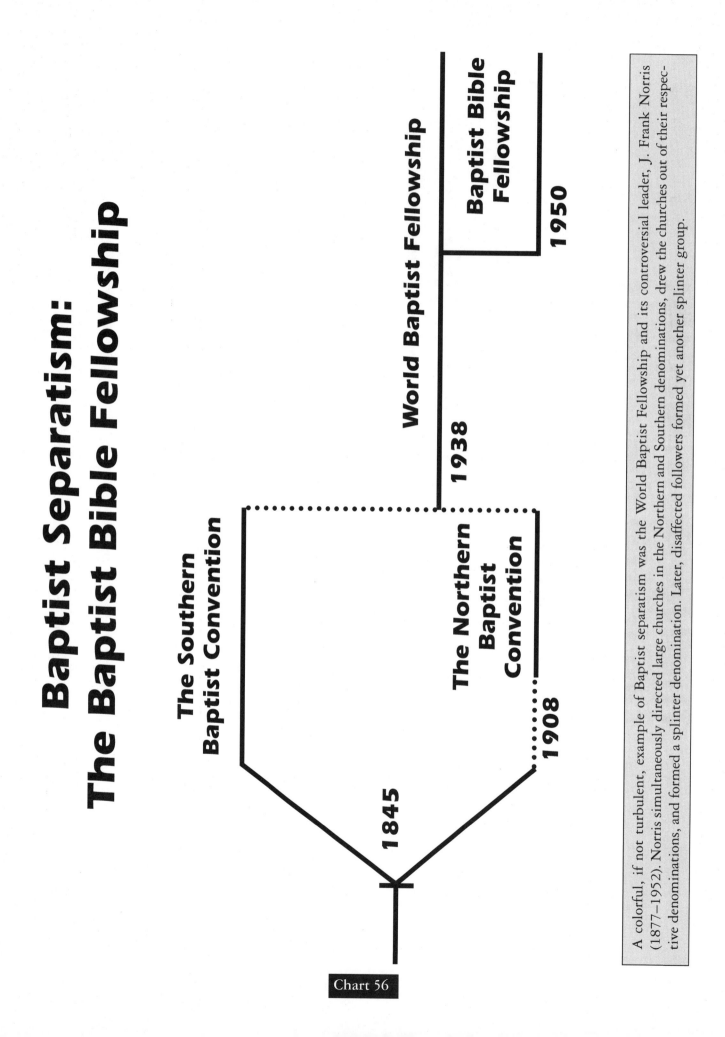

The Southern Baptist Convention

1845

The Northern Baptist Convention

1908

World Baptist Fellowship

1938

Baptist Bible Fellowship

1950

Chart 56

A colorful, if not turbulent, example of Baptist separatism was the World Baptist Fellowship and its controversial leader, J. Frank Norris (1877–1952). Norris simultaneously directed large churches in the Northern and Southern denominations, drew the churches out of their respective denominations, and formed a splinter denomination. Later, disaffected followers formed yet another splinter group.

The Methodist Separatist Movement

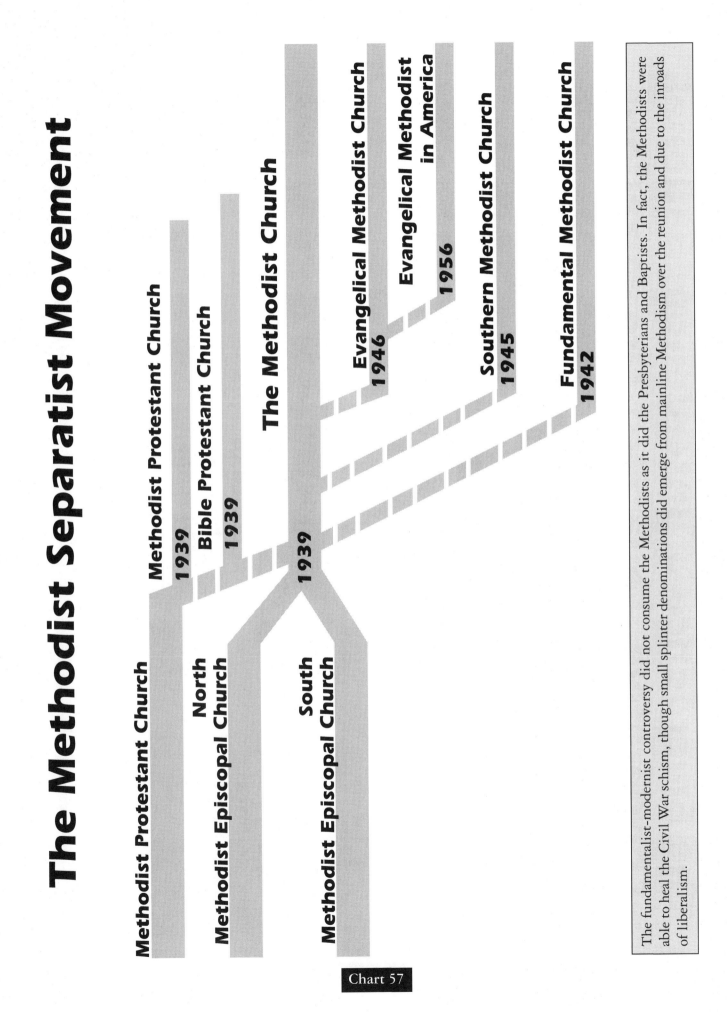

Methodist Protestant Church

Methodist Protestant Church
1939

North
Methodist Episcopal Church

Bible Protestant Church
1939

The Methodist Church

South
Methodist Episcopal Church

1939

Evangelical Methodist Church
1946

Evangelical Methodist
in America
1956

Southern Methodist Church
1945

Fundamental Methodist Church
1942

Chart 57

The fundamentalist-modernist controversy did not consume the Methodists as it did the Presbyterians and Baptists. In fact, the Methodists were able to heal the Civil War schism, though small splinter denominations did emerge from mainline Methodism over the reunion and due to the inroads of liberalism.

The Emergence of Interdenominational, Cooperative, Separatist Organizations

Chart 58

1930

Independent Fundamental Churches of America

1941

American Council of Christian Churches

1943

National Association of Evangelicals

In addition to the emergence of many conservative splinter groups from the mainline denominations, scattered evangelicals attempted to demonstrate corporate strength and unity by creating umbrella organizations for cooperative endeavors. These differed in constituencies, theological breadth, and organizational vision.

The Origins of the Independent Fundamental Churches of America

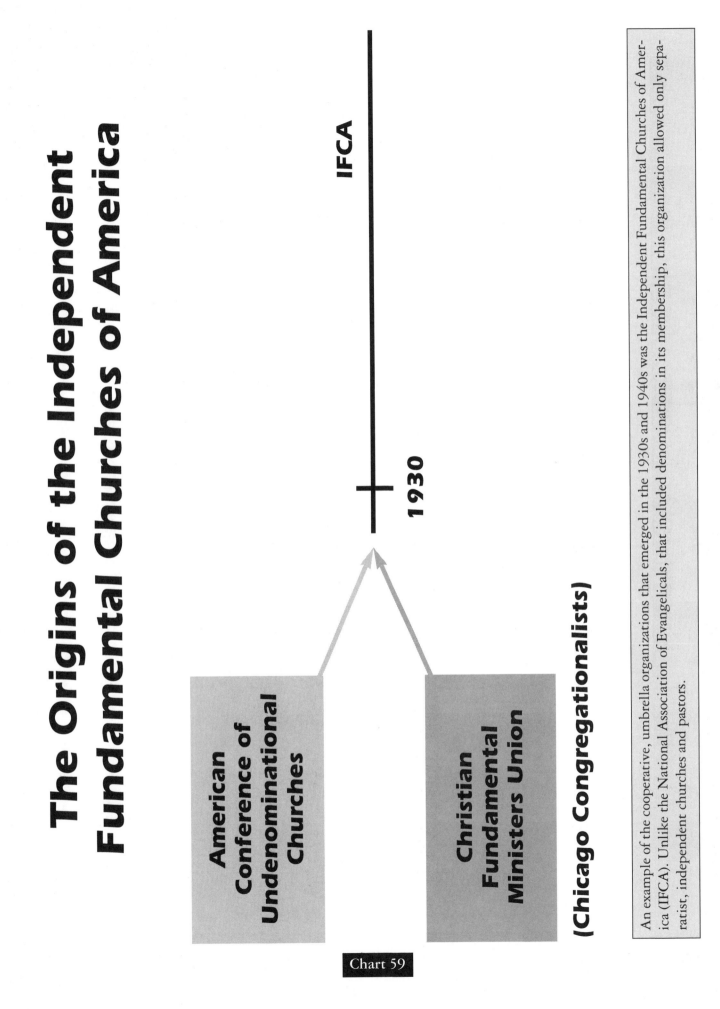

IFCA

1930

American Conference of Undenominational Churches

Christian Fundamental Ministers Union

(Chicago Congregationalists)

Chart 59

An example of the cooperative, umbrella organizations that emerged in the 1930s and 1940s was the Independent Fundamental Churches of America (IFCA). Unlike the National Association of Evangelicals, that included denominations in its membership, this organization allowed only separatist, independent churches and pastors.

The Fracturing of the Evangelical Consensus:
The Rise of New Evangelicalism

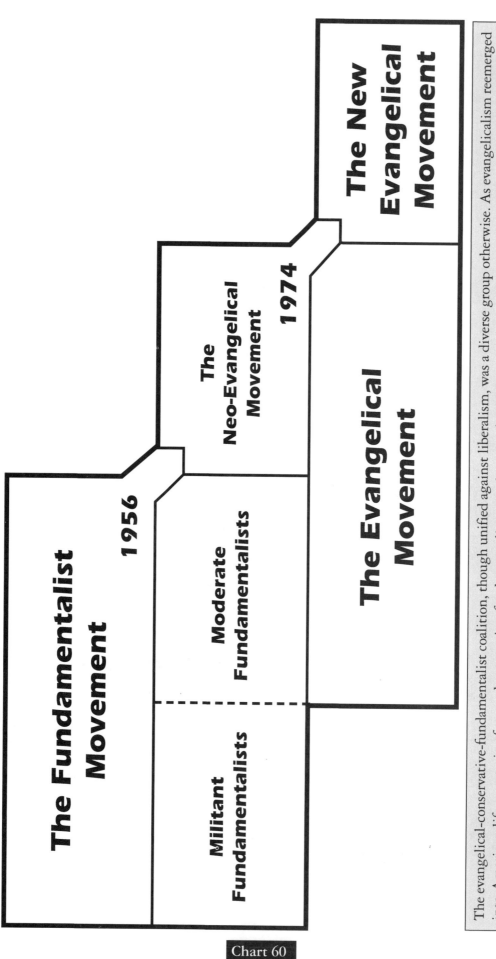

The Fundamentalist Movement

1956

Militant Fundamentalists

Moderate Fundamentalists

The Neo-Evangelical Movement

1974

The Evangelical Movement

The New Evangelical Movement

Chart 60

The evangelical-conservative-fundamentalist coalition, though unified against liberalism, was a diverse group otherwise. As evangelicalism reemerged into American life, a coterie of second-generation fundamentalists sought to make the movement more attractive and less separatistic. This new movement, neo-evangelism, splintered the group into militants, moderates, and neos. In the 1970s, a movement emerged within evangelicalism that challenged the time-held notion that biblical content was errorless. As the crisis played out, militants remained stridently opposed to liberals and concessive evangelicals, while moderates and neos coalesced. Today's spectrum within evangelical Protestantism includes the more progressive new evangelicals, moderates, and militants.

The American Liberal Impulse
in the Twentieth Century

The Shaping of Twentieth-Century Theology in America

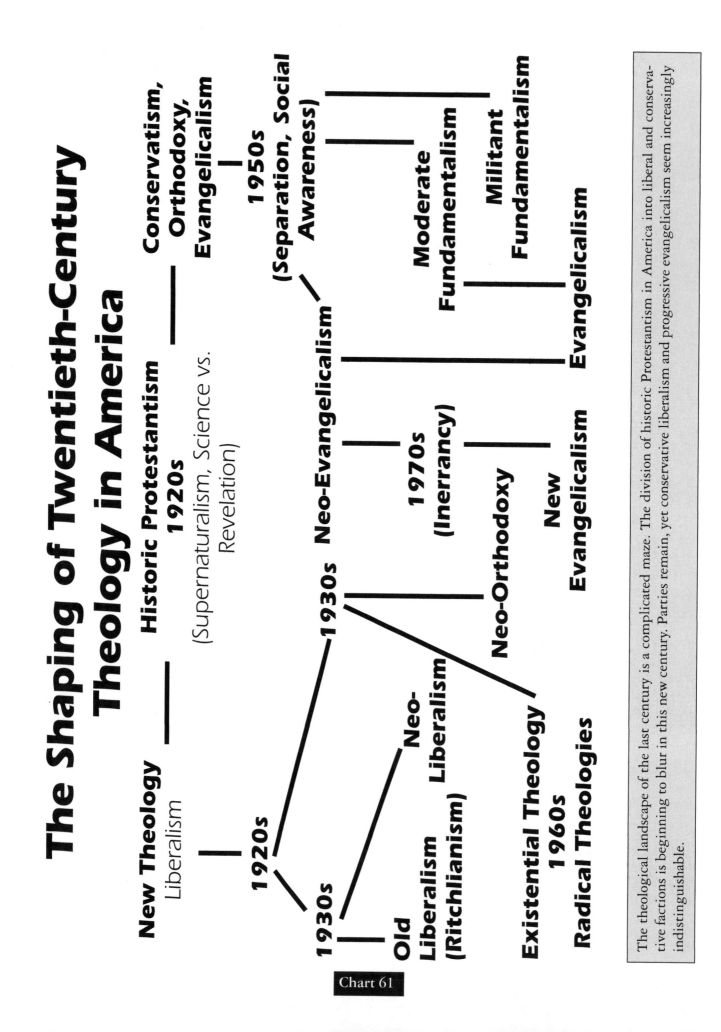

New Theology
Liberalism

Historic Protestantism
1920s
(Supernaturalism, Science vs. Revelation)

Conservatism, Orthodoxy, Evangelicalism
1950s
(Separation, Social Awareness)

1920s

1930s

Old Liberalism (Ritschlianism)

Neo-Liberalism

1930s
Neo-Evangelicalism

Neo-Orthodoxy

1970s
(Inerrancy)

Moderate Fundamentalism

Militant Fundamentalism

Existential Theology
1960s
Radical Theologies

New Evangelicalism

Evangelicalism

Chart 61

The theological landscape of the last century is a complicated maze. The division of historic Protestantism in America into liberal and conservative factions is beginning to blur in this new century. Parties remain, yet conservative liberalism and progressive evangelicalism seem increasingly indistinguishable.

The Progress of Religious Liberal Thought in America

	UNITARIANISM 1805–80	MODERNISM New Theology 1880–1930	NEO-LIBERALISM 1930–60	PROCESS THEOLOGIES 1960–
Philosophic Orientation			Realism	Idealism
Nature of Reality			Objective Being	Evolutive Becoming
Nature of Truth			Static/Moral	Emergent
World View			Mechanical	Vital
Scientific Base			Newtonian Physics	Quantum Physics
Christ			Human/Objective	Spiritual/Nonobjective

In the 1960s process theology, seeming to possess an entirely new set of assumptions and directions, became the fourth major expression of the Protestant liberal tradition in America. Some have argued that liberalism has lost its forward momentum and is fracturing into competing ideologies and goals.

Chart 62

Shapers of Religious Liberal Thought

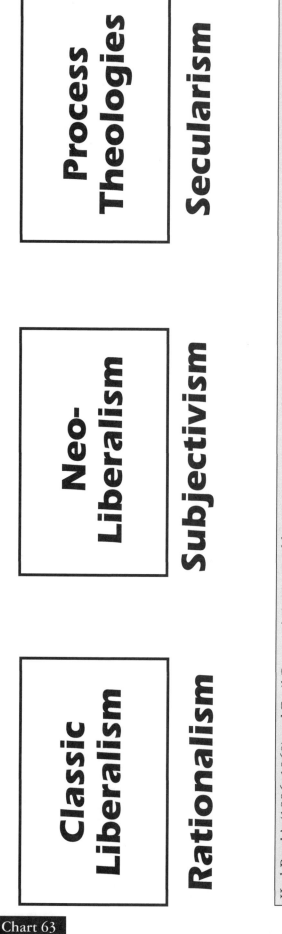

Barth
Brunner
1930

Bultmann
1960

Classic Liberalism	Neo-Liberalism	Process Theologies
Rationalism	Subjectivism	Secularism

Chart 63

Karl Barth's (1886–1968) and Emil Brunner's (1889–1966) weighty criticism of liberal progressivism and optimism influenced the emergence of a new direction in the liberal tradition. Rudolph Bultmann's (1884–1976) influence, it may be argued, caused its decline. Barth, a Swiss Reformed scholar, is considered by many the most influential theologian of the twentieth century. Not only did he offer a strident intellectual rebuke of German liberalism, he greatly impacted the rise of neo-liberalism in America as well as recent directions in evangelicalism.

Analysis of Religious Liberal Thought

"From the objective-transcendent personal God of Judeo-Christian theology, neo-Protestant interpreters have moved in recent generations to the nonobjective transcendent personal God (Barth and Brunner), to the nonobjective-transcendent, impersonal, unconditioned (Tillich), to the nonobjective-mythological-transcendent personal God (Bultmann), to nonobjective-nontranscendent religion."

Carl F. H. Henry
Frontiers in Modern Theology

Perhaps the most well known scholarly defender of evangelicalism after World War II was Carl F. H. Henry (1913–2003). In a succinct way, he summarized the drift of the liberal tradition in America.

Chart 64

The Rise of Process Theology:

The Denial of Traditional Theism

	Primordial Nature		Consequent Nature
	Abstract Transcendent		Concrete Immanent (Panentheism)
The Being Of God	Being		Becoming
The Character Of God	Directive Potentiality		Luring Actuality
The Work Of God			

Chart 65

Process theism, and the more recent emphasis in evangelicalism known as open theism, asserts that God is unchanging and changing at the same time. Proponents argue that while God is absolute in a sense, he is not sovereignly in control of events; this "divine contingence" makes God more personable, loving, and sympathetic. Nonetheless, process theism is a blatant attack on traditional notions of the God of the Bible.

The Ecumenical Movement in America

The History of the World Council of Churches

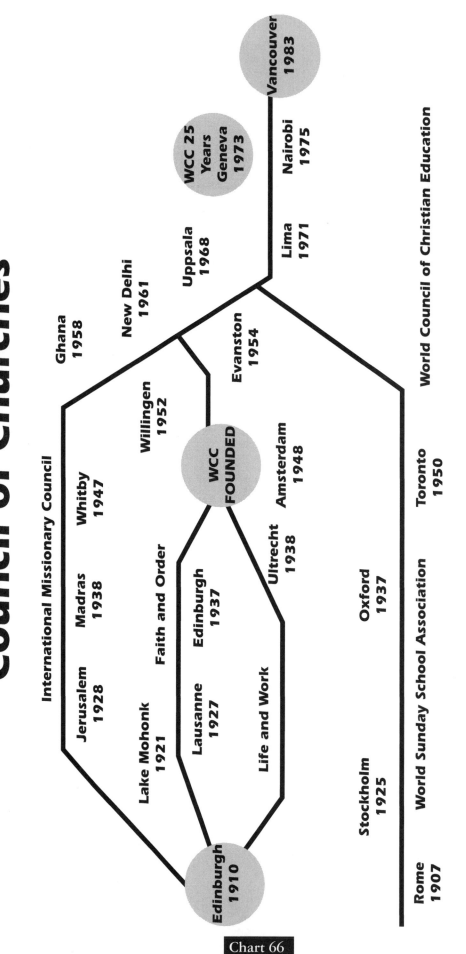

International Missionary Council

Ghana 1958

New Delhi 1961

Uppsala 1968

WCC 25 Years Geneva 1973

Nairobi 1975

Lima 1971

Vancouver 1983

Jerusalem 1928

Madras 1938

Whitby 1947

Lake Mohonk 1921

Faith and Order

Willingen 1952

Evanston 1954

Lausanne 1927

Edinburgh 1937

WCC FOUNDED

Life and Work

Ultrecht 1938

Amsterdam 1948

Stockholm 1925

Oxford 1937

Toronto 1950

Rome 1907

World Sunday School Association

World Council of Christian Education

Edinburgh 1910

Chart 66

The World Council of Churches is an ecumenical group of Protestant and orthodox churches worldwide. It purposes to extend the Christian witness through mission and service by cooperative enterprise. Membership includes over three hundred denominations in a hundred countries. Though not an official member, the Roman Catholic Church participates in the Commission on Faith and Order.

The History of the American Ecumenical Movement

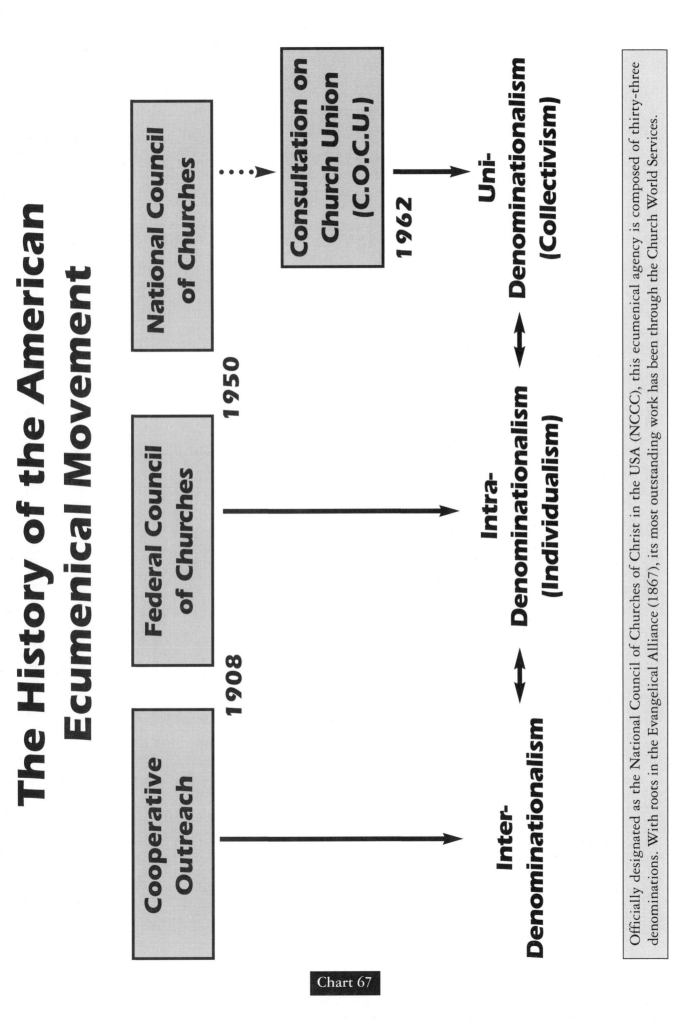

Cooperative Outreach

Federal Council of Churches

National Council of Churches

Consultation on Church Union (C.O.C.U.)

1908

1950

1962

Inter-Denominationalism

Intra-Denominationalism (Individualism)

Uni-Denominationalism (Collectivism)

Chart 67

Controversies within Mainline Denominations and Their Current State

The Southern Baptist Convention and the Fundamentalist Controversy

Toy Case	Norris Controversy	Elliot Case	Broadman Controversy
1870s	1920s	1960s	1970s

Chart 68

The Southern Baptist Convention, created in 1845, has struggled since the 1870s over the authority of Scripture. This recurring issue has remained unresolved and is the root of the fundamentalist-moderate controversy of the past several decades. Even so, the SBC is the largest Protestant denomination in America with over fifteen million members in over forty-one thousand churches.

The Political Structure within the Southern Baptist Convention

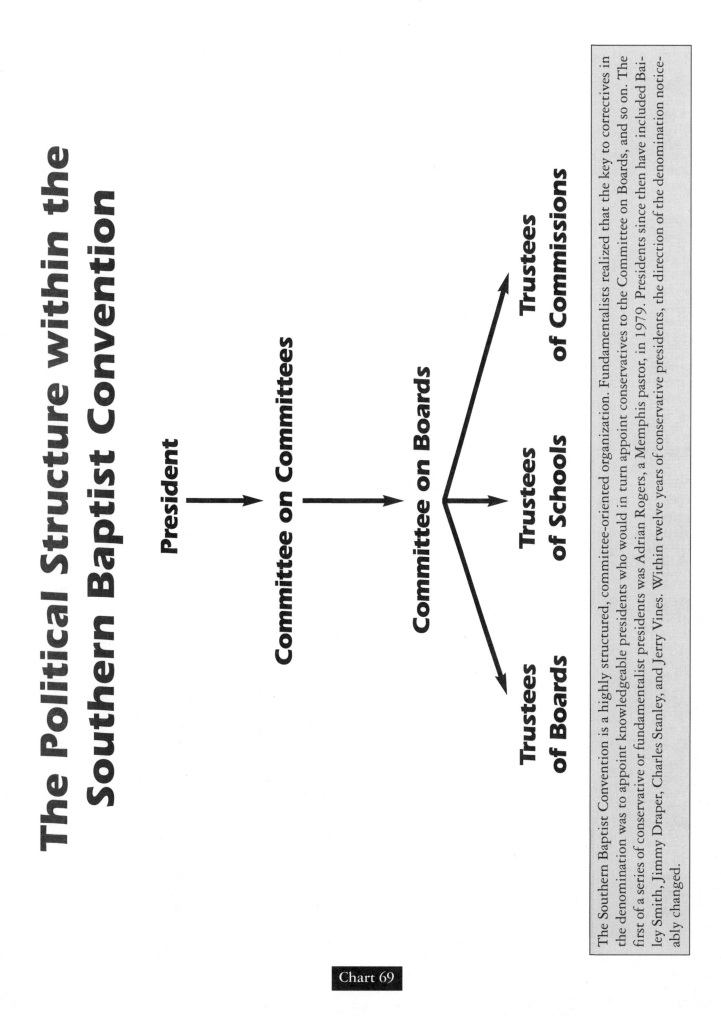

President

↓

Committee on Committees

↓

Committee on Boards

Trustees of Boards   Trustees of Schools   Trustees of Commissions

The Southern Baptist Convention is a highly structured, committee-oriented organization. Fundamentalists realized that the key to correctives in the denomination was to appoint knowledgeable presidents who would in turn appoint conservatives to the Committee on Boards, and so on. The first of a series of conservative or fundamentalist presidents was Adrian Rogers, a Memphis pastor, in 1979. Presidents since then have included Bailey Smith, Jimmy Draper, Charles Stanley, and Jerry Vines. Within twelve years of conservative presidents, the direction of the denomination noticeably changed.

Chart 69

The Northern Baptist Convention Today

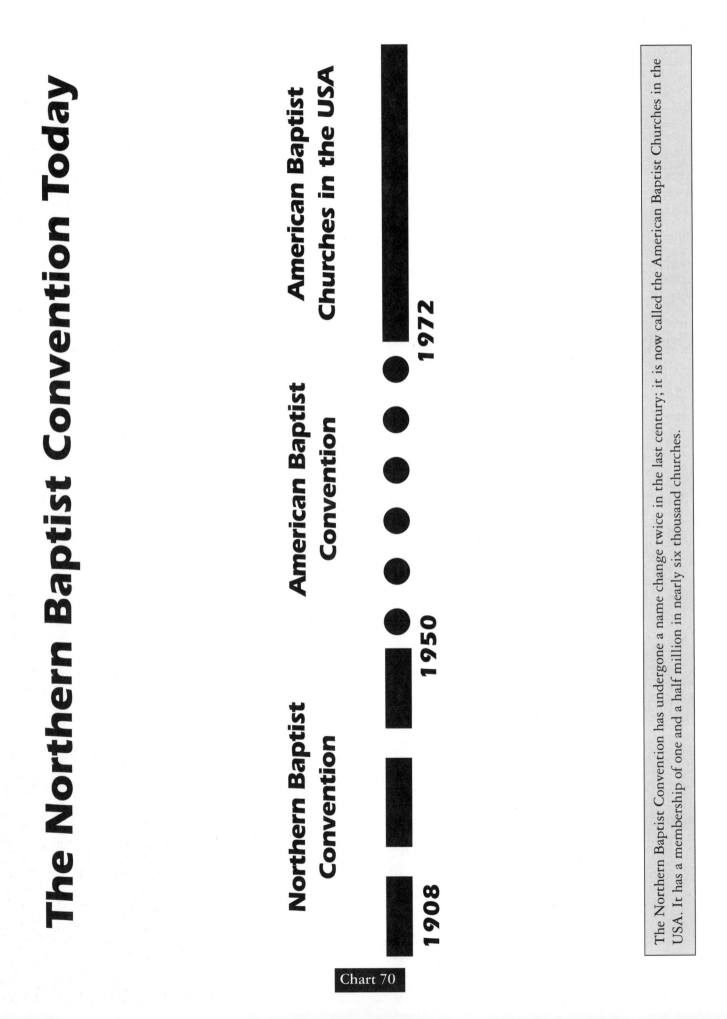

Northern Baptist
Convention

American Baptist
Convention

American Baptist
Churches in the USA

1908   1950   1972

Chart 70

The Northern Baptist Convention has undergone a name change twice in the last century; it is now called the American Baptist Churches in the USA. It has a membership of one and a half million in nearly six thousand churches.

The History of the Presbyterian Church in America

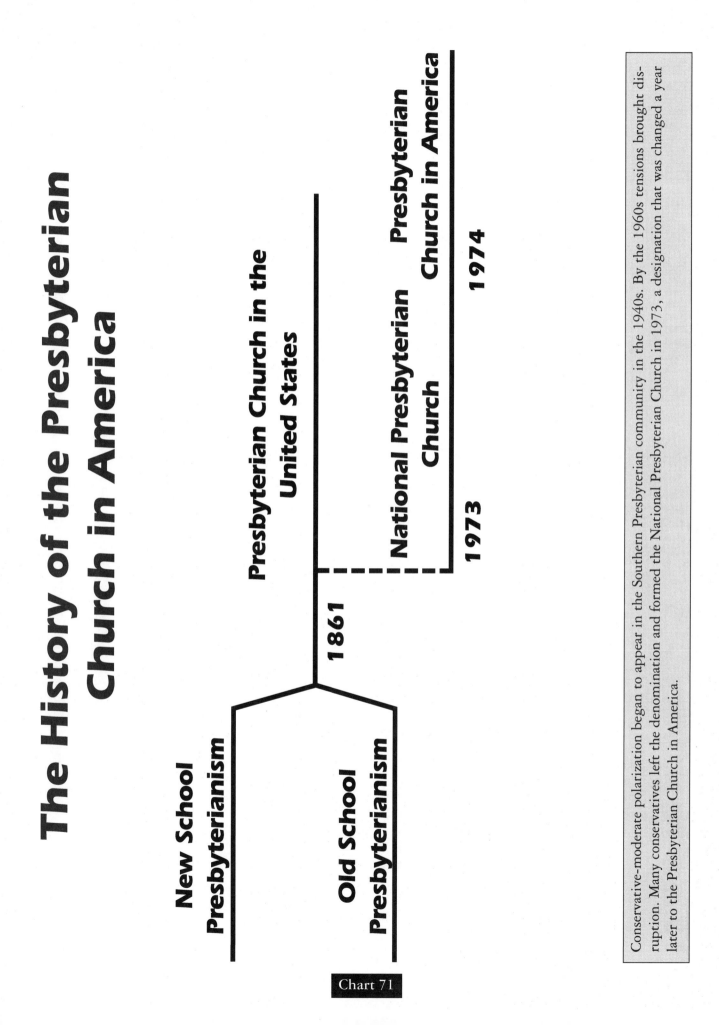

New School Presbyterianism

Presbyterian Church in the United States

Old School Presbyterianism

1861

National Presbyterian Church

Presbyterian Church in America

1973

1974

Chart 71

Conservative-moderate polarization began to appear in the Southern Presbyterian community in the 1940s. By the 1960s tensions brought disruption. Many conservatives left the denomination and formed the National Presbyterian Church in 1973, a designation that was changed a year later to the Presbyterian Church in America.

The Presbyterian Church in America Today

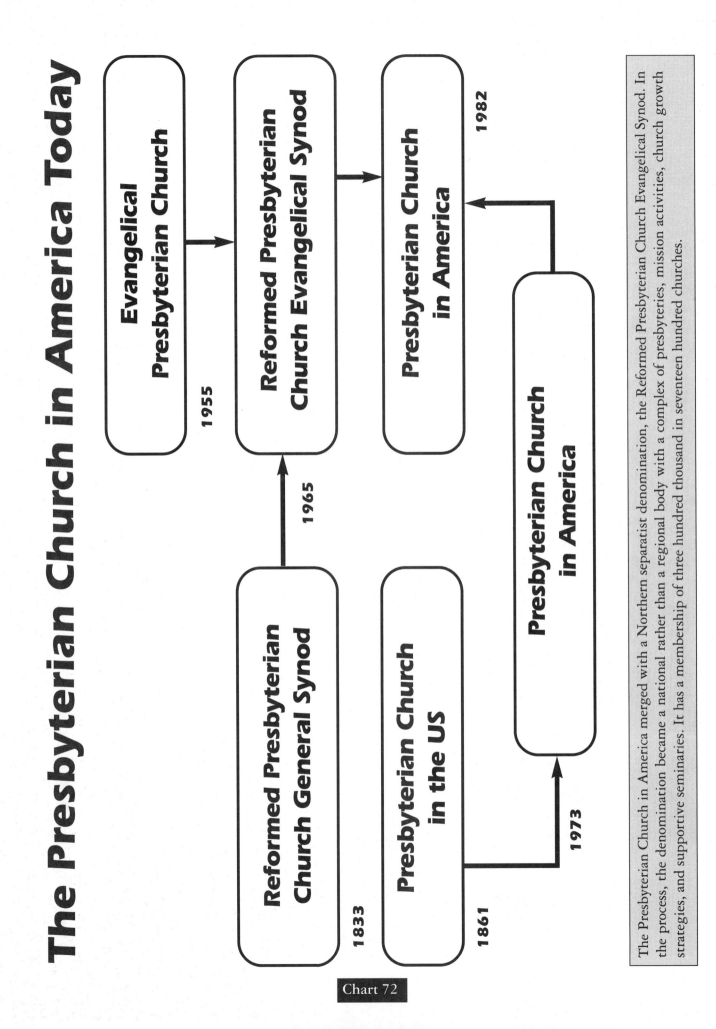

Evangelical Presbyterian Church — 1955

Reformed Presbyterian Church Evangelical Synod — 1965

Presbyterian Church in America — 1982

Reformed Presbyterian Church General Synod — 1833

Presbyterian Church in the US — 1861

Presbyterian Church in America — 1973

Chart 72

The Presbyterian Church in America merged with a Northern separatist denomination, the Reformed Presbyterian Church Evangelical Synod. In the process, the denomination became a national rather than a regional body with a complex of presbyteries, mission activities, church growth strategies, and supportive seminaries. It has a membership of three hundred thousand in seventeen hundred churches.

The Presbyterian Church, USA

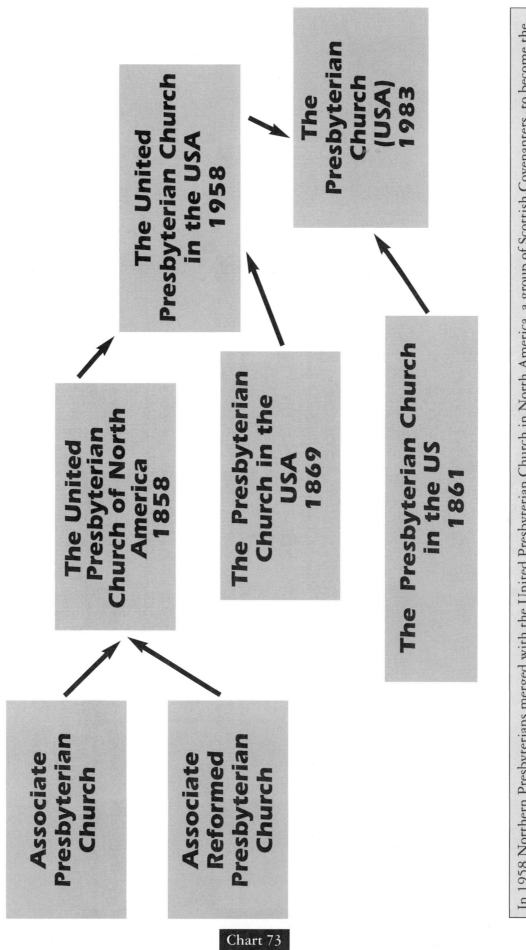

Associate Presbyterian Church

Associate Reformed Presbyterian Church

The United Presbyterian Church of North America 1858

The Presbyterian Church in the USA 1869

The Presbyterian Church in the US 1861

The United Presbyterian Church in the USA 1958

The Presbyterian Church (USA) 1983

Chart 73

In 1958 Northern Presbyterians merged with the United Presbyterian Church in North America, a group of Scottish Covenanters, to become the United Presbyterian Church in the USA. Then in 1983 the Northern church merged with the Southern church to become the Presbyterian Church (USA). The PCUSA has a membership of three and a half million in eleven thousand churches.

The History of the Methodist Church (1830–1939)

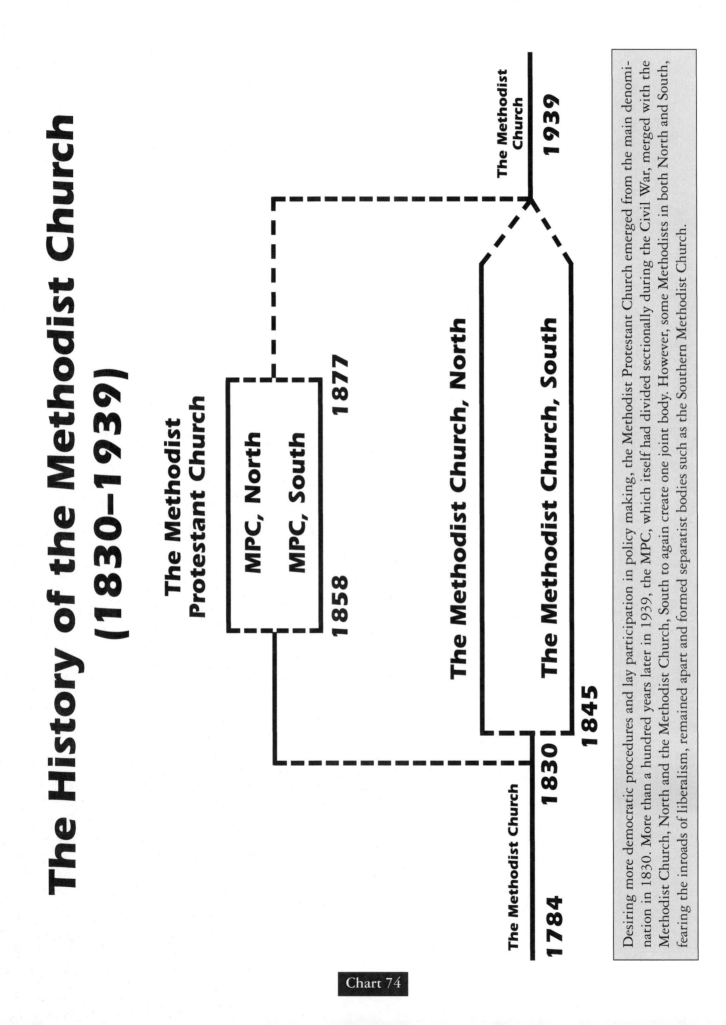

The Methodist
Protestant Church

MPC, North

MPC, South

The Methodist Church

1784   1830

1845

The Methodist Church, North

The Methodist Church, South

1858   1877

The Methodist
Church

1939

Desiring more democratic procedures and lay participation in policy making, the Methodist Protestant Church emerged from the main denomination in 1830. More than a hundred years later in 1939, the MPC, which itself had divided sectionally during the Civil War, merged with the Methodist Church, North and the Methodist Church, South to again create one joint body. However, some Methodists in both North and South, fearing the inroads of liberalism, remained apart and formed separatist bodies such as the Southern Methodist Church.

Chart 74

The Creation of the United Methodist Church

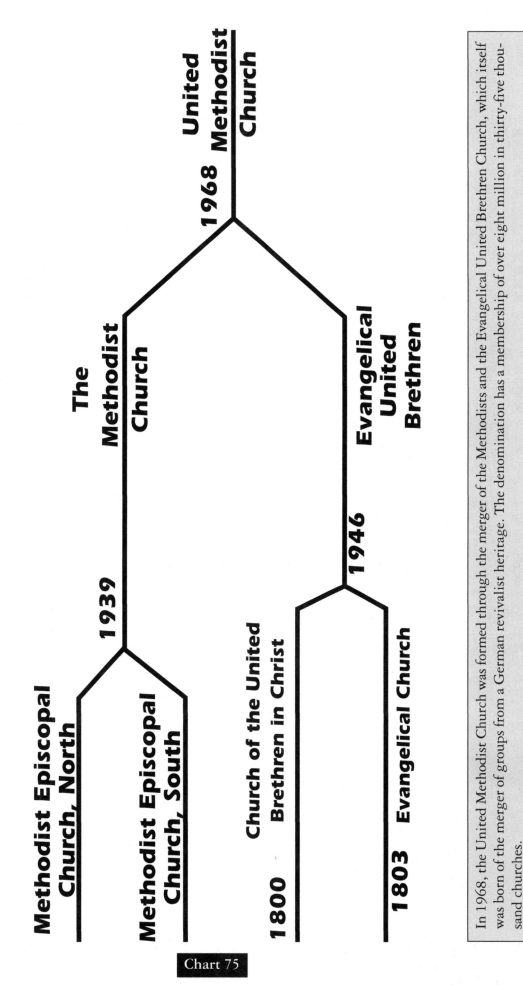

Methodist Episcopal Church, North

Methodist Episcopal Church, South

1939 → The Methodist Church

Church of the United Brethren in Christ

1800

1803 Evangelical Church

1946 → Evangelical United Brethren

1968 → United Methodist Church

Chart 75

In 1968, the United Methodist Church was formed through the merger of the Methodists and the Evangelical United United Brethren Church, which itself was born of the merger of groups from a German revivalist heritage. The denomination has a membership of over eight million in thirty-five thousand churches.

The History of Congregationalism in the Twentieth Century:

The Congregational Christian Churches

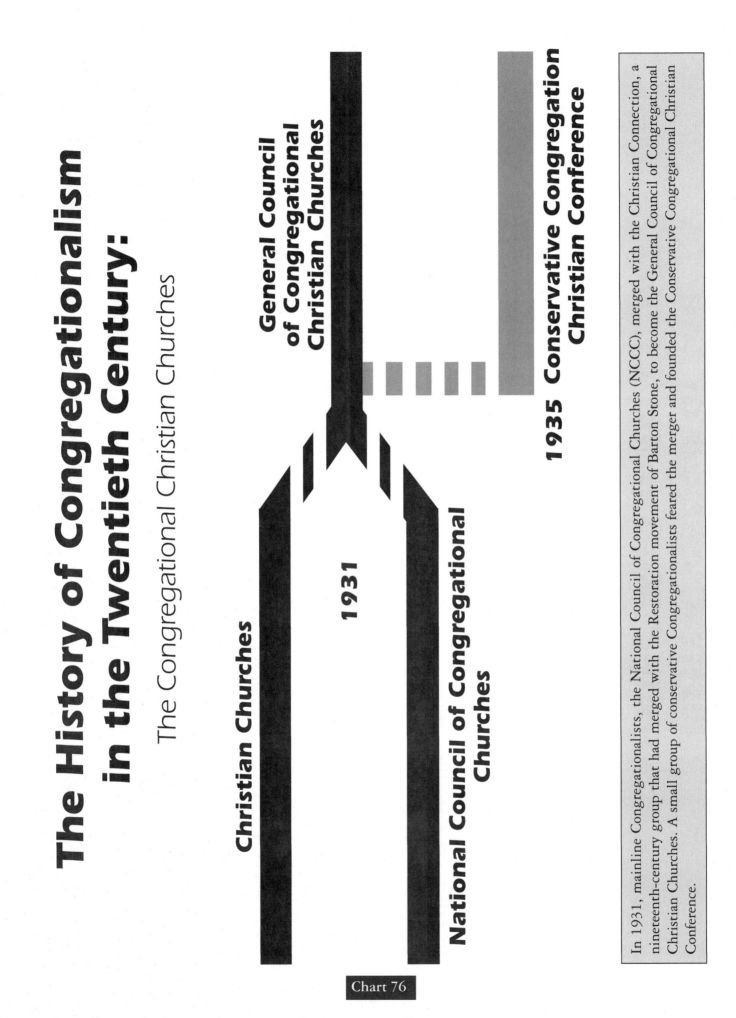

Christian Churches

General Council of Congregational Christian Churches

1931

National Council of Congregational Churches

1935 Conservative Congregation Christian Conference

In 1931, mainline Congregationalists, the National Council of Congregational Churches (NCCC), merged with the Restoration movement of Barton Stone, a nineteenth-century group that had merged with the Christian Connection, to become the General Council of Congregational Christian Churches. A small group of conservative Congregationalists feared the merger and founded the Conservative Congregational Christian Conference.

Chart 76

The United Church of Christ

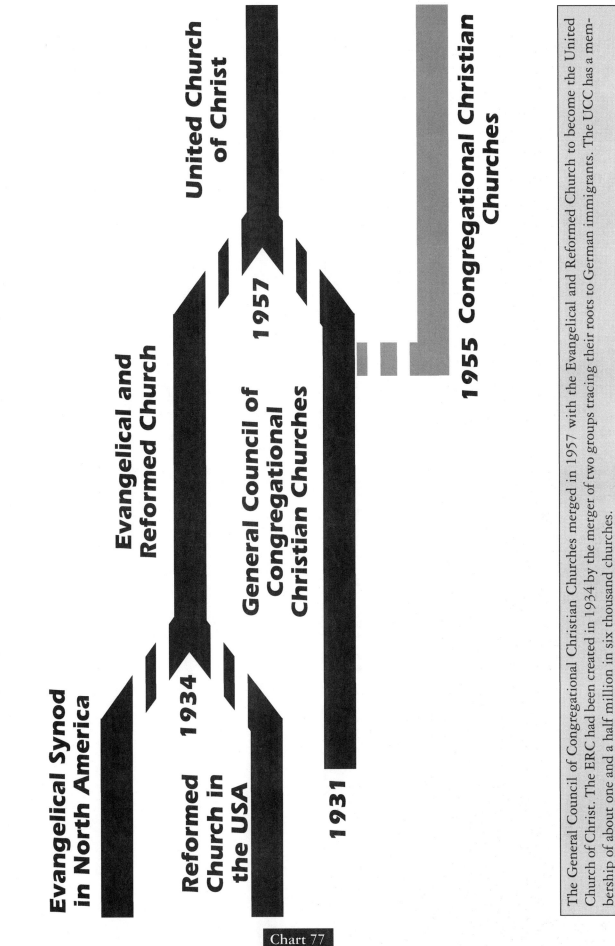

Evangelical Synod
in North America

Evangelical and
Reformed Church

Reformed
Church in
the USA

1934

General Council of
Congregational
Christian Churches

1931

United Church
of Christ

1957

1955 Congregational Christian
Churches

Chart 77

The General Council of Congregational Christian Churches merged in 1957 with the Evangelical and Reformed Church to become the United Church of Christ. The ERC had been created in 1934 by the merger of two groups tracing their roots to German immigrants. The UCC has a membership of about one and a half million in six thousand churches.

The Lutheran Church, Missouri Synod and the Association of Evangelical Lutheran Churches

Lutheran Church, Missouri Synod

1847

Lutheran Church, Missouri Synod

Association of Evangelical Lutheran Churches

1976

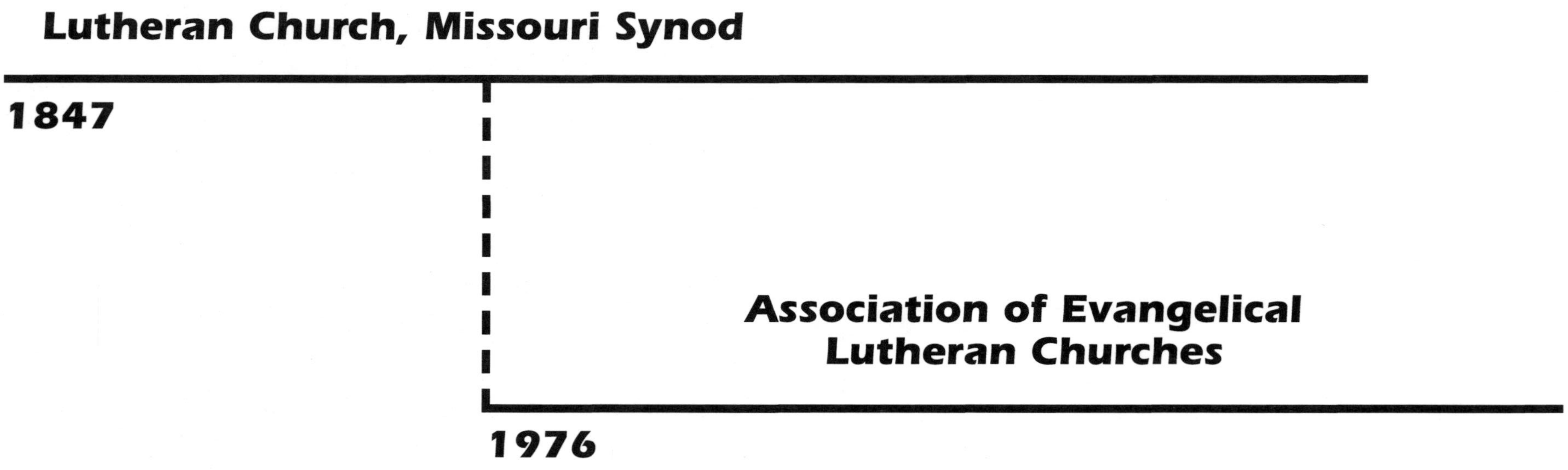

Conservative-liberal tensions flared in the Lutheran Church, Missouri Synod in the 1960s and 1970s, mostly surrounding the direction of the denomination's primary seminary, Concordia, in St. Louis. The struggle became increasingly intense at denominational meetings and conservatives won a resounding victory. Consequently, moderates withdrew, forming a separatist denomination, the Association of Evangelical Lutheran Churches (AELC). The LCMS has a membership of over two and a half million in over six thousand churches.

Chart 78

The Evangelical Lutheran Church in America

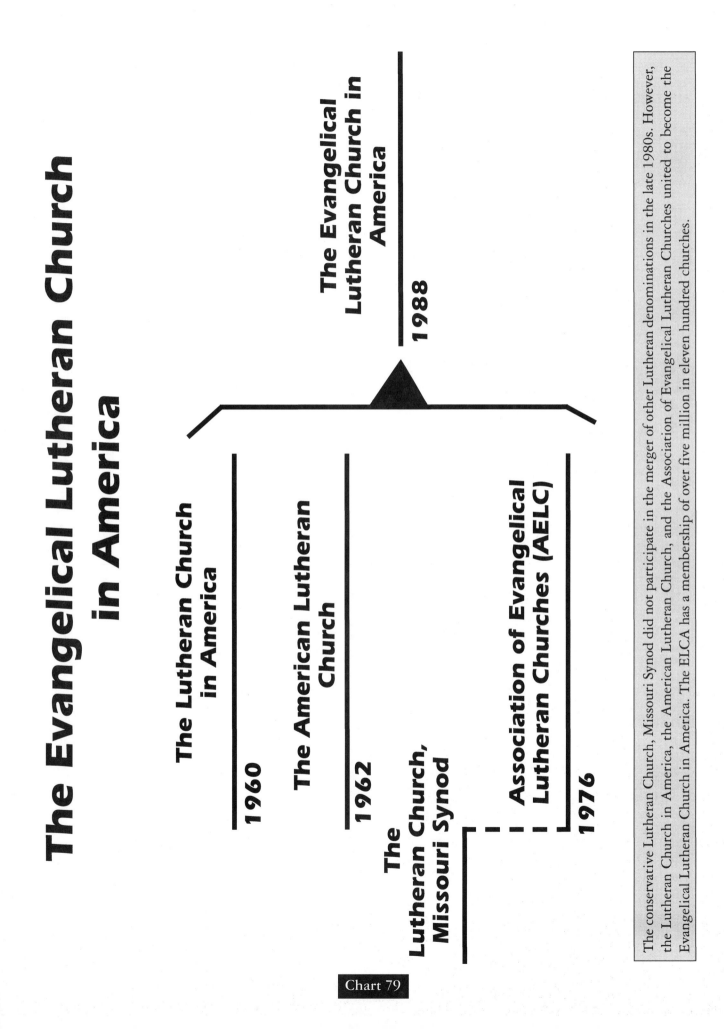

The Lutheran Church in America

1960

The American Lutheran Church

1962

The Lutheran Church, Missouri Synod

Association of Evangelical Lutheran Churches (AELC)

1976

The Evangelical Lutheran Church in America

1988

The conservative Lutheran Church, Missouri Synod did not participate in the merger of other Lutheran denominations in the late 1980s. However, the Lutheran Church in America, the American Lutheran Church, and the Association of Evangelical Lutheran Churches united to become the Evangelical Lutheran Church in America. The ELCA has a membership of over five million in eleven hundred churches.

Chart 79

The History of the Episcopal Church in the USA

The Church
of England

Protestant Episcopal
Church in the USA

The Episcopal Church
in the USA (ECUSA)

1785

1967

Chart 80

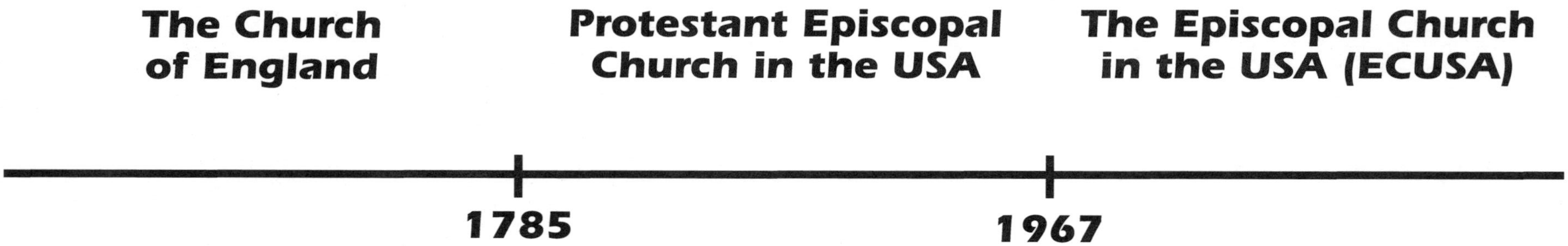

Though still part of the Anglican community worldwide, after the Revolutionary War American church leaders broke with the Church of England and organized along more nationalistic lines, renaming themselves the Protestant Episcopal Church. In the late nineteenth century, those worried by liberal inroads formed the Reformed Episcopal Church. Then in 1967 the Protestant Episcopal Church was renamed the Episcopal Church in the USA (ECUSA). The denomination experienced a decline in membership between 1965 and 1975, but has stabilized since the mid-1980s.

Polarization within the Episcopal Church, USA

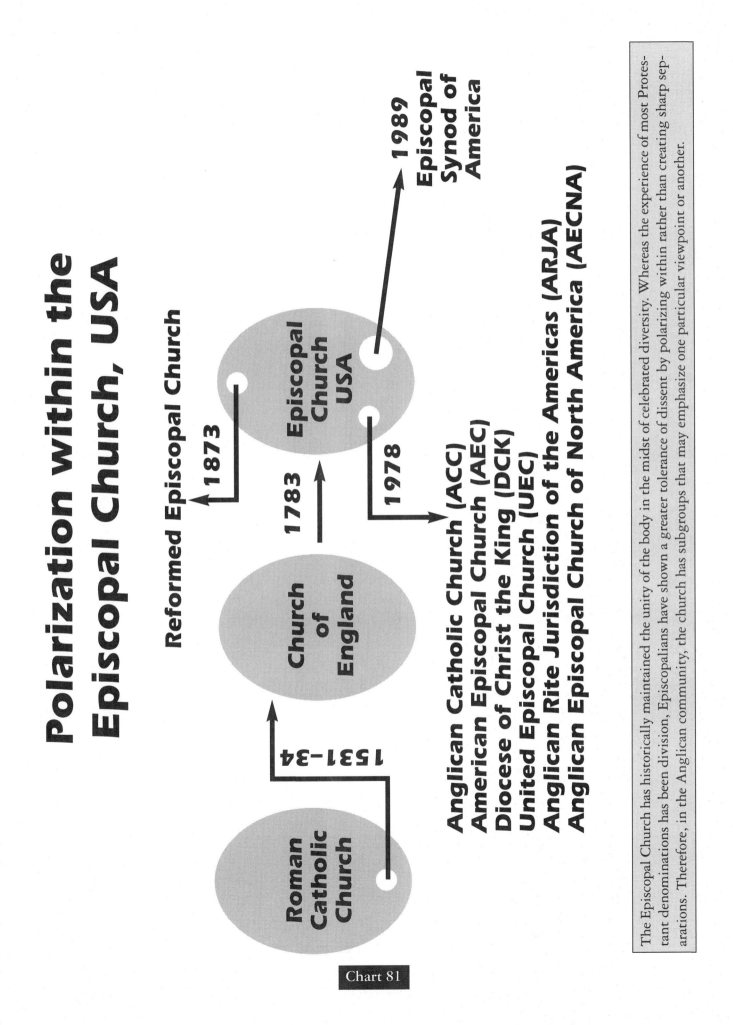

Reformed Episcopal Church

1873

Episcopal Church USA

1783

Church of England

1531-34

Roman Catholic Church

1978

Anglican Catholic Church (ACC)
American Episcopal Church (AEC)
Diocese of Christ the King (DCK)
United Episcopal Church (UEC)
Anglican Rite Jurisdiction of the Americas (ARJA)
Anglican Episcopal Church of North America (AECNA)

1989
Episcopal Synod of America

Chart 81

The Episcopal Church has historically maintained the unity of the body in the midst of celebrated diversity. Whereas the experience of most Protestant denominations has been division, Episcopalians have shown a greater tolerance of dissent by polarizing within rather than creating sharp separations. Therefore, in the Anglican community, the church has subgroups that may emphasize one particular viewpoint or another.

Numerical Decline
in the Mainline Churches

Denomination	Decline in 1970s–80s	Decline from 1990–2003
American Baptist Church	+6.6%	-7% (106,739 people)
Episcopal Church	-17%	-5% (12,095 people)
Disciples of Christ (Christian Church)	-29%	-27% (189,551 people)
Presbyterian Church, USA	-25%	-15% (435,827 people)
United Church of Christ	-16%	-17% (258,680 people)
United Methodist Church	-13%	-8% (751,430 people)

Sources: *Quarterly Review*, Fall 1987 and *Yearbook of American and Canadian Churches*, 1986, 1990, 2003

Chart 82

Numerical losses of most mainline denominations at the close of the last century were staggering. Statistics support the thesis that cultural accommodation left the churches without a distinctive message or defining passion, leading to increasing disinterest among parishioners and eventual departure. However, denominations such as the Assemblies of God and the Southern Baptist Convention, which refused to waver theologically, continued to grow.

Select Important Evangelical Groups in America Today

The Associate Reformed Presbyterian Church, General Synod

Chart 83

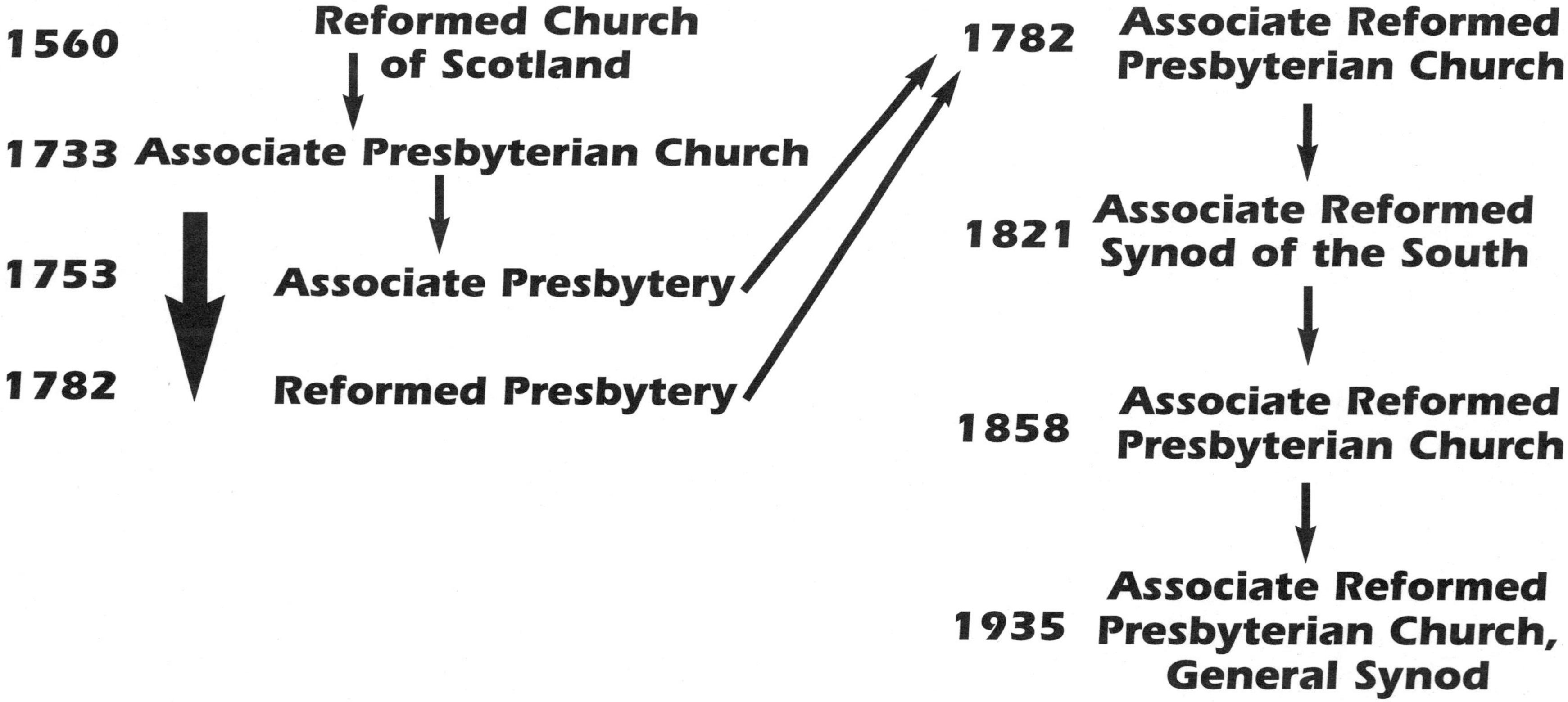

1560 Reformed Church of Scotland

1733 Associate Presbyterian Church

1753 Associate Presbytery

1782 Reformed Presbytery

1782 Associate Reformed Presbyterian Church

1821 Associate Reformed Synod of the South

1858 Associate Reformed Presbyterian Church

1935 Associate Reformed Presbyterian Church, General Synod

The Associate Reformed Presbyterian Church, General Synod has its roots in the Church of Scotland; it is "covenanter" in origin and tradition. The denomination follows the Westminster Confession of Faith as its standard. There are some forty thousand members in about two hundred forty churches, with a college and seminary in South Carolina.

The Evangelical Presbyterian Church

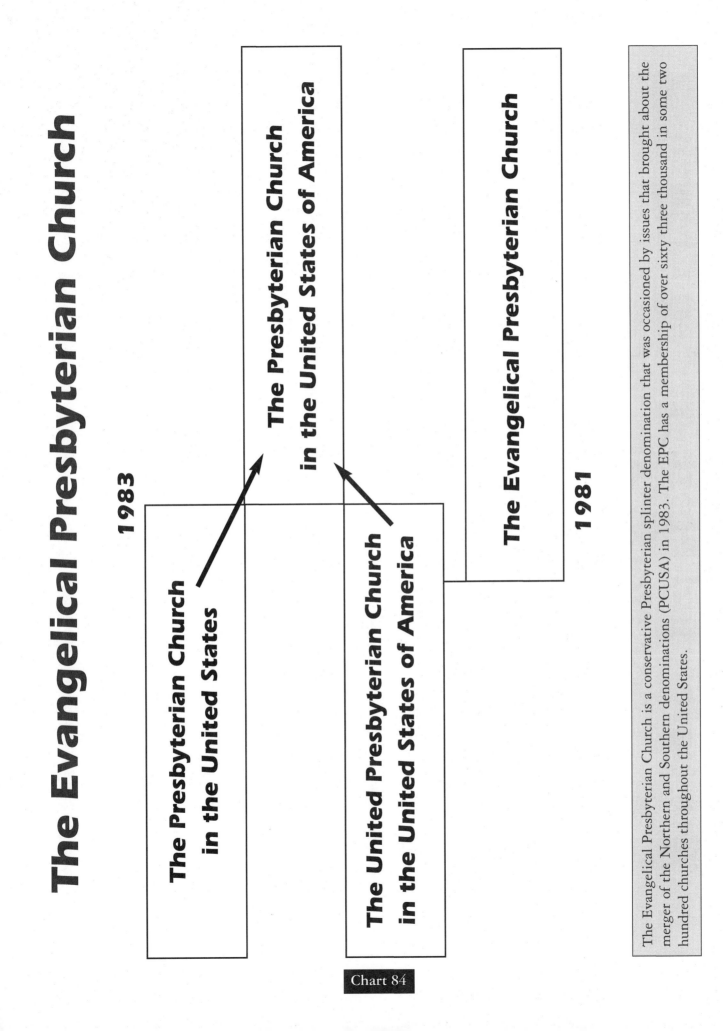

1983

The Presbyterian Church
in the United States

The Presbyterian Church
in the United States of America

The United Presbyterian Church
in the United States of America

The Evangelical Presbyterian Church

1981

Chart 84

The Evangelical Presbyterian Church is a conservative Presbyterian splinter denomination that was occasioned by issues that brought about the merger of the Northern and Southern denominations (PCUSA) in 1983. The EPC has a membership of over sixty three thousand in some two hundred churches throughout the United States.

The Reformed Presbyterian Church of North America

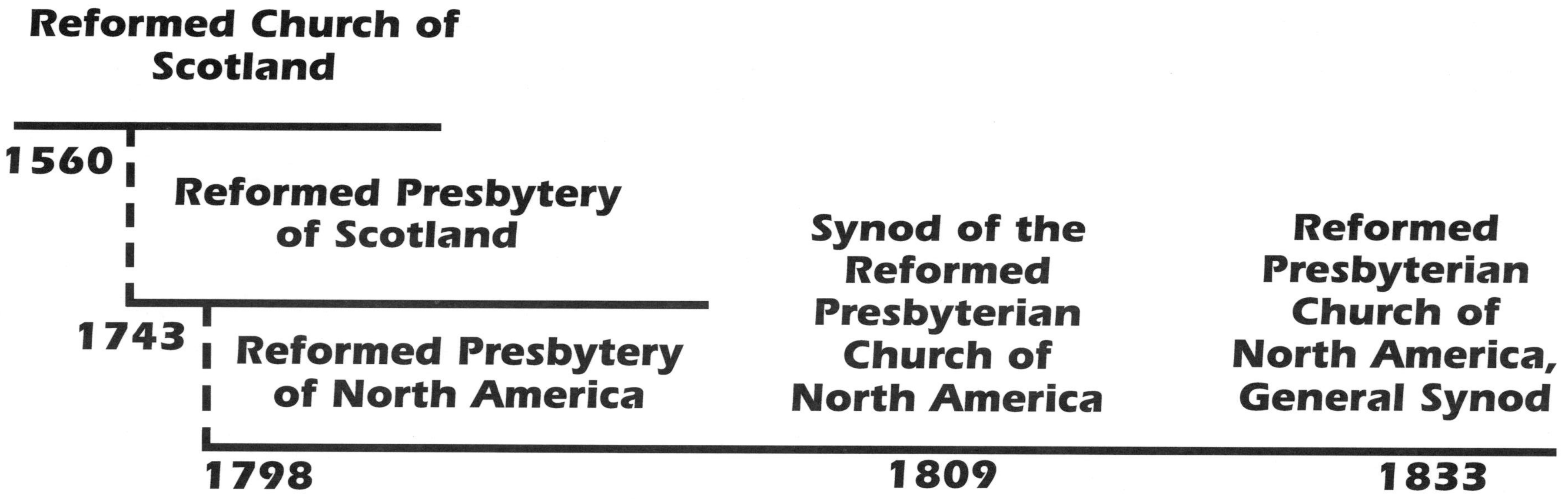

Reformed Church of Scotland

1560

Reformed Presbytery of Scotland

1743

Reformed Presbytery of North America

1798

Synod of the Reformed Presbyterian Church of North America

1809

Reformed Presbyterian Church of North America, General Synod

1833

Chart 85

The Reformed Presbyterian Church of North America is rooted in the Scottish covenanter tradition. The denomination emerged over debate about the biblical legitimacy of the federal constitution. The RPCNA argued that while the constitution was defective, it was not immoral and that voting in national elections is not a violation of the covenant. The church is a confessional community subscribing to the Westminster Confession of Faith. It practices closed communion, does not permit musical instruments in worship, and sings only the psalms. The church consists of about six thousand members in about ninety churches.

The Baptist General Conference

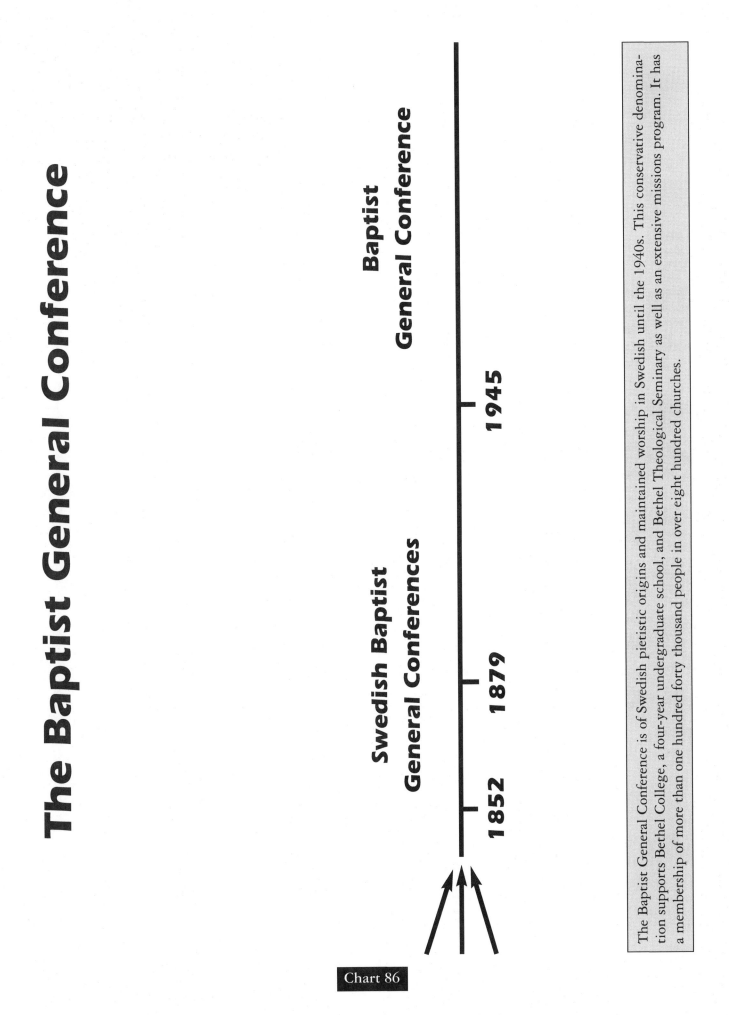

Swedish Baptist
General Conferences

1852   1879

Baptist
General Conference

1945

Chart 86

The Baptist General Conference is of Swedish pietistic origins and maintained worship in Swedish until the 1940s. This conservative denomination supports Bethel College, a four-year undergraduate school, and Bethel Theological Seminary as well as an extensive missions program. It has a membership of more than one hundred forty thousand people in over eight hundred churches.

The National Association of Free Will Baptists

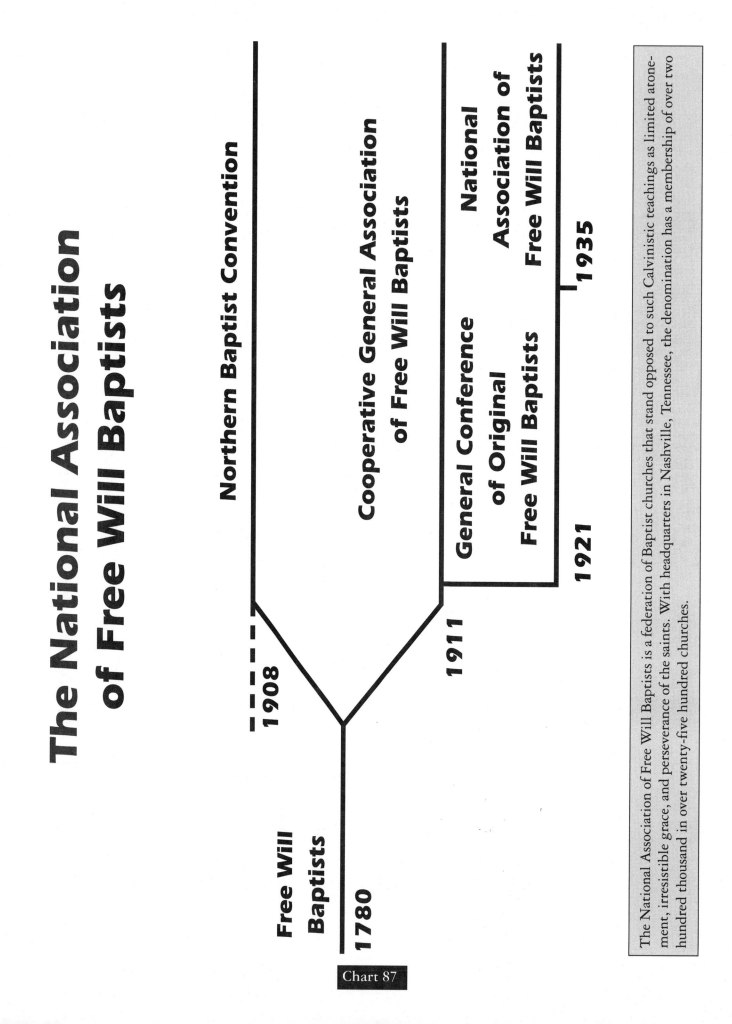

Free Will Baptists — 1780

Northern Baptist Convention — 1908

Cooperative General Association of Free Will Baptists — 1911

General Conference of Original Free Will Baptists — 1921

National Association of Free Will Baptists — 1935

Chart 87

The National Association of Free Will Baptists is a federation of Baptist churches that stand opposed to such Calvinistic teachings as limited atonement, irresistible grace, and perseverance of the saints. With headquarters in Nashville, Tennessee, the denomination has a membership of over two hundred thousand in over twenty-five hundred churches.

The Reformed Church in America

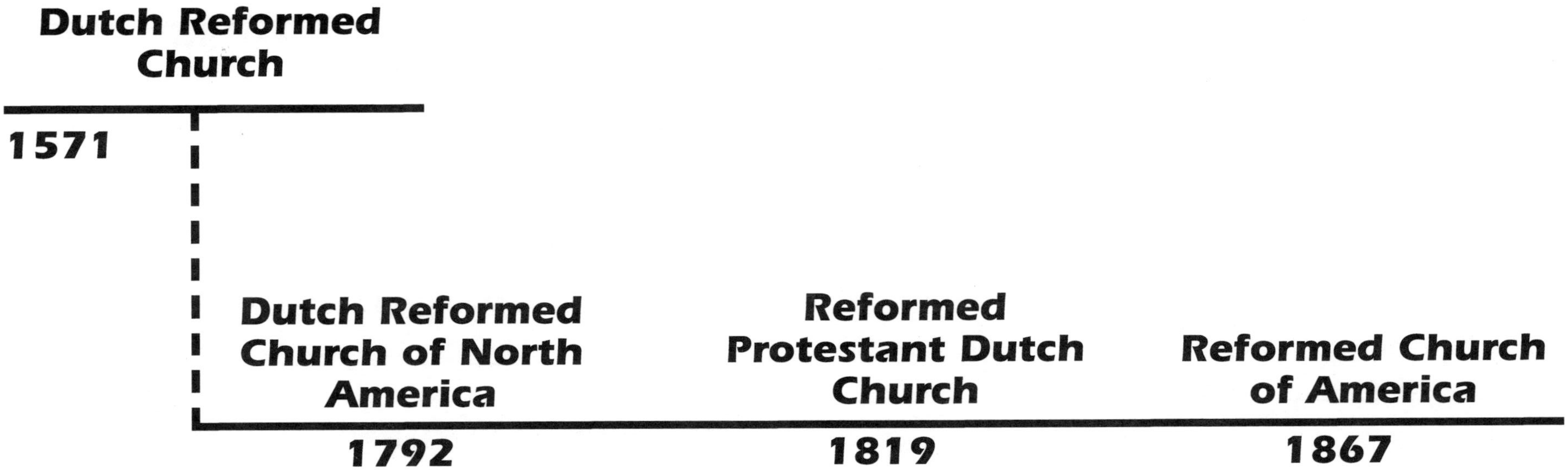

Dutch Reformed Church

1571

Dutch Reformed Church of North America

1792

Reformed Protestant Dutch Church

1819

Reformed Church of America

1867

Chart 88

The Reformed Church in America was formally organized in 1792 of Dutch immigrants who had settled in New York and northern New Jersey. The church officially subscribes to three great standards: the Belgic Confession, the Heidelberg Catechism, and the Synod of Dordt. The denomination has about nine hundred churches with a membership of over three hundred thousand and has most recently focused on social issues and matters of national policy.

The Christian Reformed Church

1819   Reformed Protestant Dutch Church → Holland Reformed Church

Reformed Church of America 1867

1857   Holland Reformed Church →

1861   True Dutch Reformed Church →

1880   Holland Christian Reformed Church in America →

1890   Christian Reformed Church in America →

1904   Christian Reformed Church

Chart 89

The Christian Reformed Church is of Dutch and Reformed origins, with its geographical center in Grand Rapids, Michigan. This conservative denomination has three colleges: Calvin College, Dordt College, and Trinity College. It has a membership in excess of two hundred thousand in over seven hundred churches.

The Evangelical Covenant Church

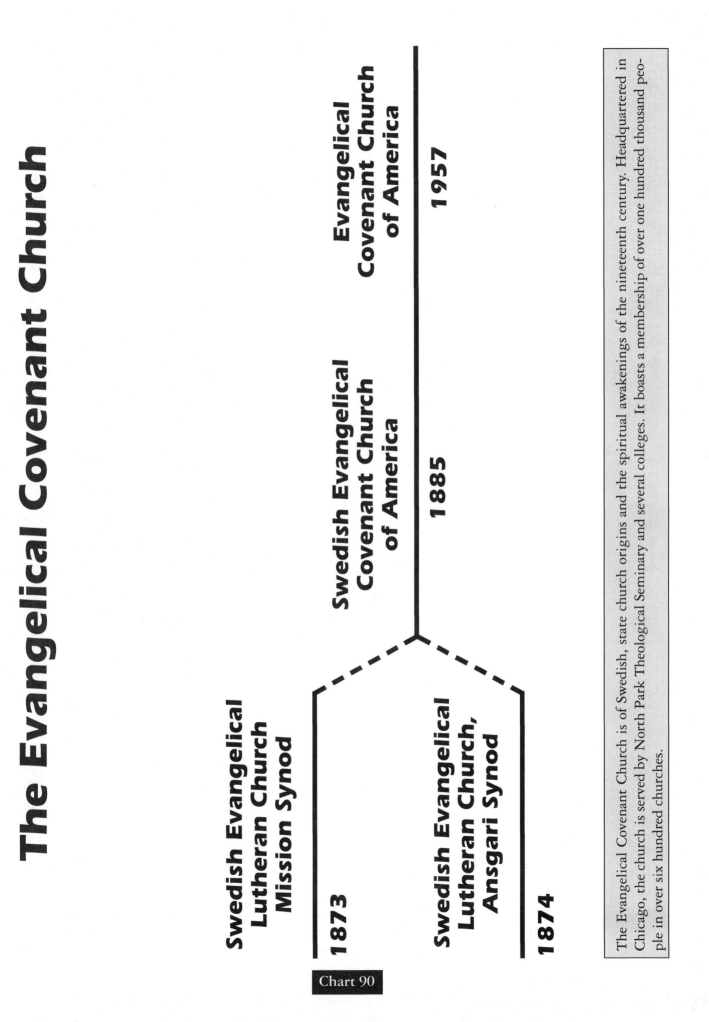

Swedish Evangelical
Lutheran Church
Mission Synod

1873

Swedish Evangelical
Lutheran Church,
Ansgari Synod

1874

Swedish Evangelical
Covenant Church
of America

1885

Evangelical
Covenant Church
of America

1957

Chart 90

The Evangelical Covenant Church is of Swedish, state church origins and the spiritual awakenings of the nineteenth century. Headquartered in Chicago, the church is served by North Park Theological Seminary and several colleges. It boasts a membership of over one hundred thousand people in over six hundred churches.

The Evangelical Free Church of America

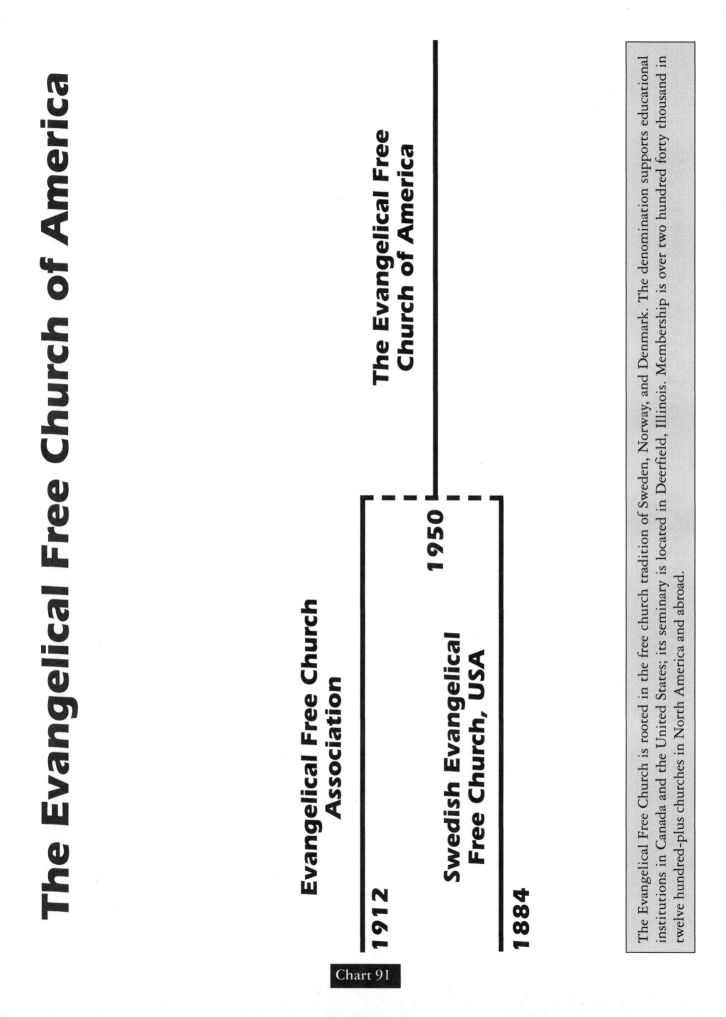

Evangelical Free Church Association

1912

Swedish Evangelical Free Church, USA

1884

1950

The Evangelical Free Church of America

Chart 91

The Evangelical Free Church is rooted in the free church tradition of Sweden, Norway, and Denmark. The denomination supports educational institutions in Canada and the United States; its seminary is located in Deerfield, Illinois. Membership is over two hundred forty thousand in twelve hundred-plus churches in North America and abroad.

The Free Methodist Church of North America

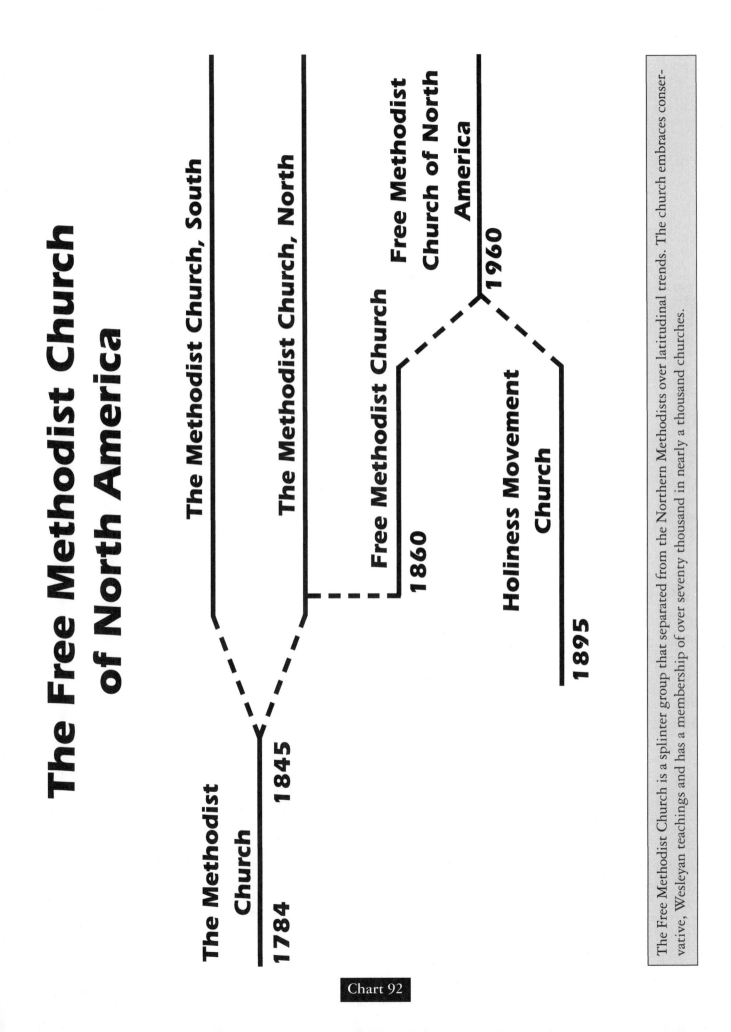

The Methodist Church, South

The Methodist Church, North

Free Methodist Church of North America

1960

Free Methodist Church

1860

Holiness Movement Church

1895

The Methodist Church

1784   1845

Chart 92

The Free Methodist Church is a splinter group that separated from the Northern Methodists over latitudinal trends. The church embraces conservative, Wesleyan teachings and has a membership of over seventy thousand in nearly a thousand churches.

The Wesleyan Church

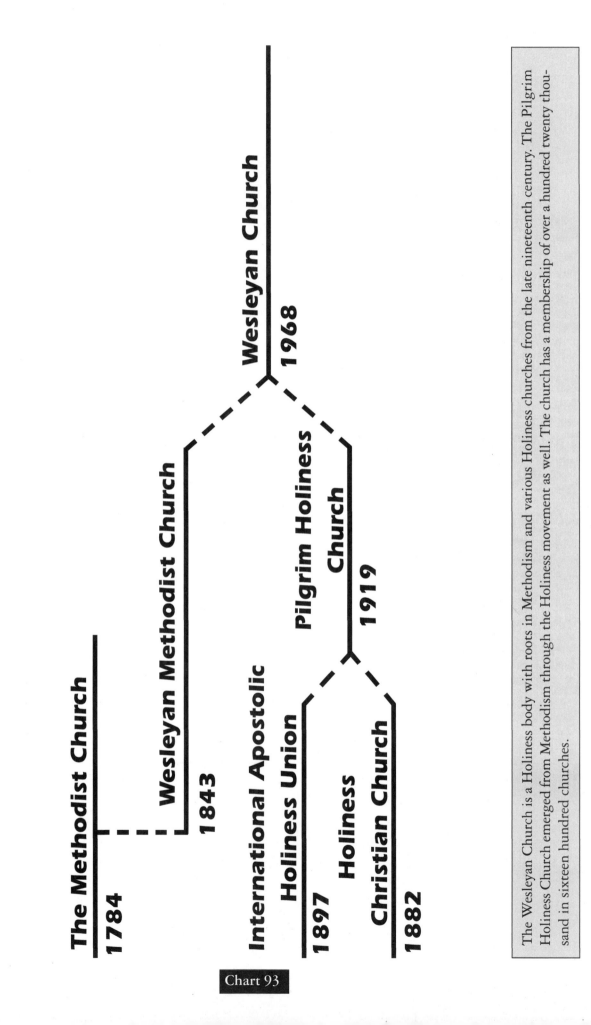

The Methodist Church
1784

Wesleyan Methodist Church
1843

International Apostolic Holiness Union
1897

Holiness Christian Church
1882

Pilgrim Holiness Church
1919

Wesleyan Church
1968

Chart 93

The Wesleyan Church is a Holiness body with roots in Methodism and various Holiness churches from the late nineteenth century. The Pilgrim Holiness Church emerged from Methodism through the Holiness movement as well. The church has a membership of over a hundred twenty thousand in sixteen hundred churches.

The Brethren Churches

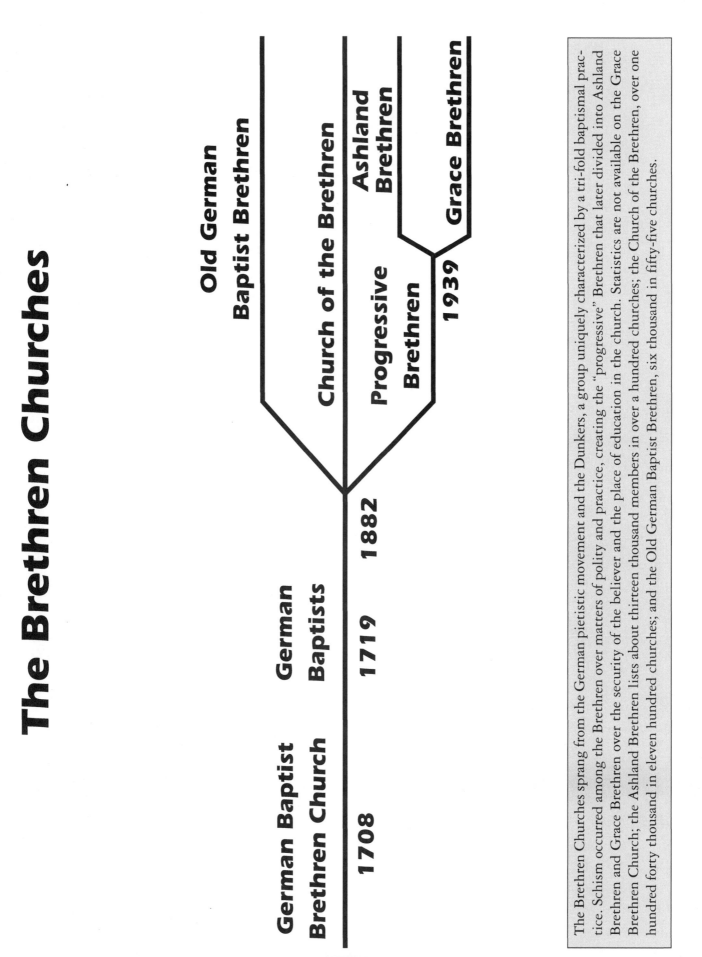

Chart 94

German Baptist Brethren Church 1708

German Baptists 1719

Old German Baptist Brethren

1882

Church of the Brethren

Progressive Brethren

Ashland Brethren

1939

Grace Brethren

The Brethren Churches sprang from the German pietistic movement and the Dunkers, a group uniquely characterized by a tri-fold baptismal practice. Schism occurred among the Brethren over matters of polity and practice, creating the "progressive" Brethren that later divided into Ashland Brethren and Grace Brethren over the security of the believer and the place of education in the church. Statistics are not available on the Grace Brethren Church; the Ashland Brethren lists about thirteen thousand members in over a hundred churches; the Church of the Brethren, over one hundred forty thousand in eleven hundred churches; and the Old German Baptist Brethren, six thousand in fifty-five churches.

The State of Roman
Catholicism in America

The Roman Catholic Church in the Nineteenth Century:
The Initial Struggle to Maintain Orthodoxy

1854 **The Immaculate Conception of Mary Dogmatized**

1869–70 **Vatican I**
(a) Defense against liberalism

(b) Syllabus of error

(c) Dogmatizing of papal infallibility

"When he speaks ex cathedra, that is, when in discharge of the office of pastor and doctor of all Christians . . . he . . . is possessed of that infallibility with which the divine Redeemer willed."
Session 4:4

In the mid-nineteenth century the Roman Catholic Church declared that Mary was conceived without the influence of sin and, therefore, was sinless. A decade and a half later, in reaction to liberal trends, the church called Vatican I, which listed intolerable errors. This effectively drove dissent underground, where it festered for over a century. Vatican I also clarified papal powers, pronouncing the pope's authority to speak binding truth in his official capacity.

Chart 95

The Roman Catholic Church and the Ongoing Struggle to Preserve Orthodoxy

1963–65   **Vatican II**
(An openness to Protestant ecumenicism)
Protestants = "errant brethren"
Dialogue with other faiths encouraged
Bible translation and reading permitted
Mass in vernacular and lay participation

1967   **The Duquene weekend and the beginning of charismatic renewalism**

1968   **"Humanae Vitae"**
(The condemnation of artificial means of contraception)

1978   **John Paul II**   **Personal charm**
Theological traditionalism
Selective pragmatism

1994   **The catechism of the Catholic Church (a restatement of traditional theology)**

Vatican II brought some significant changes to the church, though not the substantive loosening of doctrinal narrowism that many sought. The church embraced and assimilated the charismatic movement and in John Paul II has a leader committed to traditional moral and doctrinal views.

Chart 96

The Popes Since Vatican I

Pius IX (1845–78)	**Vatican I, "Syllabus of Errors," infallibility**
Leo III (1878–1903)	
Pius X (1903–14)	**Return to Pius IX's ways "New Syllabus of Errors"**
Benedict XV (1914–22)	**World War I**
Pius XI (1922–39)	**Encyclical against birth control**
Pius XII (1939–58)	**Anti-modernist, anti-semitic, pronounced the dogma of Mary's assumption**
John XXIII (1958–63)	**A progressive pope, called Vatican II to reform the church**
Paul VI (1963–78)	**Traditional pope, Anti-modernist**
John Paul I (1978)	
John Paul II (1978–present)	**Anti-modernist, traditionalist, sainted Pius IX (2000)**

An ongoing theme in the Roman Catholic Church, as in Protestant churches, has been a struggle against the destructive assault of rationalism on traditional teachings. Most of the popes in the past century and a half have been anti-modernist (pejoratively called medievalists). They have attempted to resist recent trends in theology and practice with little success.

Chart 97

The African-American Church

The History of the Modern Civil Rights Movement

The Principle of Equality: *Implied*

The Principle of Equality: *Stated*

The Principle of Equality: *Applied*

Declaration of Independence	Civil Rights Amendments 13 & 15	Brown vs. Board of Ed.	Civil Rights Act	Voting Rights Act
1776	1865, 1870	1954	1964	1965

Desegregation of Public Schools

Chart 98

There have been three remarkable moments in the American struggle for minority rights. The principle of equality was implied in our great documents of state, expressed in the amendments to the Constitution following the Civil War, and became a reality in the Civil Rights movement of the 1950s and 1960s.

The Phases of the Modern Civil Rights Movement

Phase I: Desegregation (Public Places)

Phase II: Voting (Ballot Box)

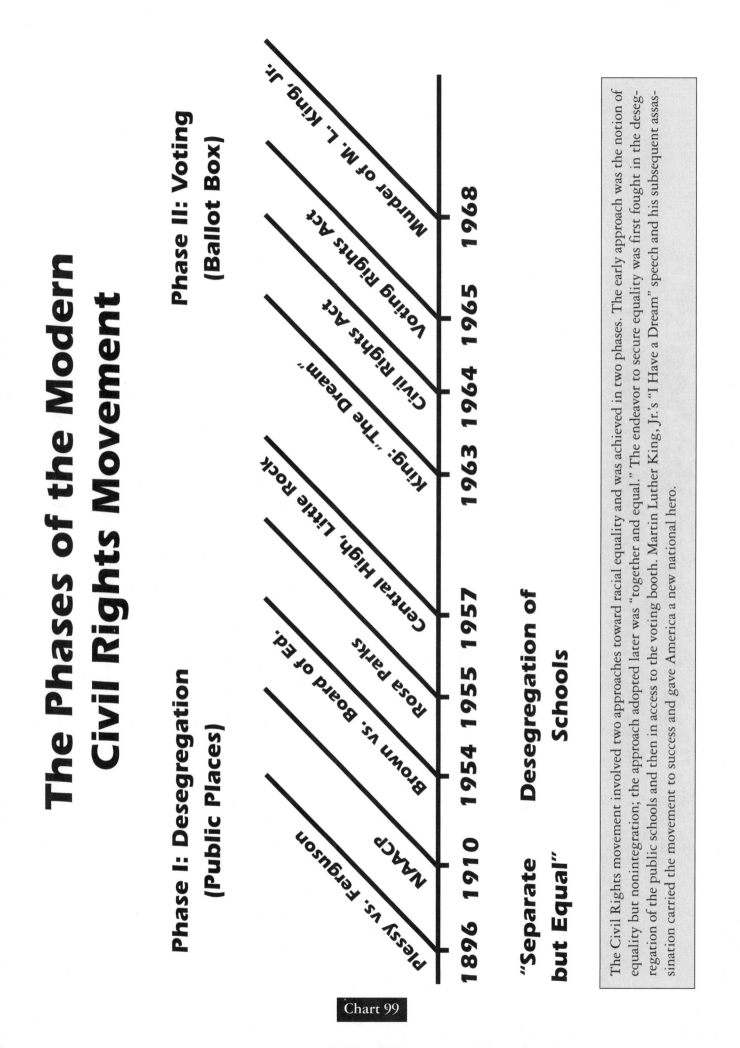

Plessy vs. Ferguson — 1896

NAACP — 1910

Brown vs. Board of Ed. — 1954

Rosa Parks — 1955

Central High, Little Rock — 1957

King: "The Dream" — 1963

Civil Rights Act — 1964

Voting Rights Act — 1965

Murder of M. L. King, Jr. — 1968

"Separate but Equal"   Desegregation of Schools

Chart 99

The Civil Rights movement involved two approaches toward racial equality and was achieved in two phases. The early approach was the notion of equality but nonintegration; the approach adopted later was "together and equal." The endeavor to secure equality was first fought in the desegregation of the public schools and then in access to the voting booth. Martin Luther King, Jr.'s "I Have a Dream" speech and his subsequent assassination carried the movement to success and gave America a new national hero.

The African Methodist Episcopal Zion Church

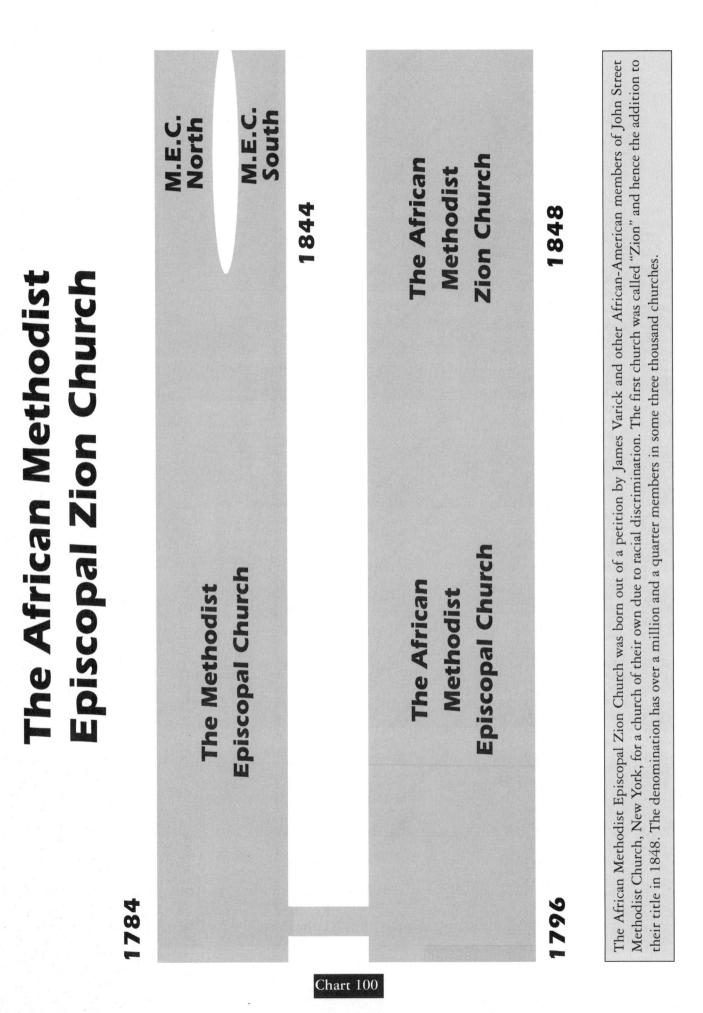

1784

The Methodist Episcopal Church

M.E.C. North

M.E.C. South

1844

1796

The African Methodist Episcopal Church

The African Methodist Zion Church

1848

The African Methodist Episcopal Zion Church was born out of a petition by James Varick and other African-American members of John Street Methodist Church, New York, for a church of their own due to racial discrimination. The first church was called "Zion" and hence the addition to their title in 1848. The denomination has over a million and a quarter members in some three thousand churches.

Chart 100

The African Methodist Episcopal Church

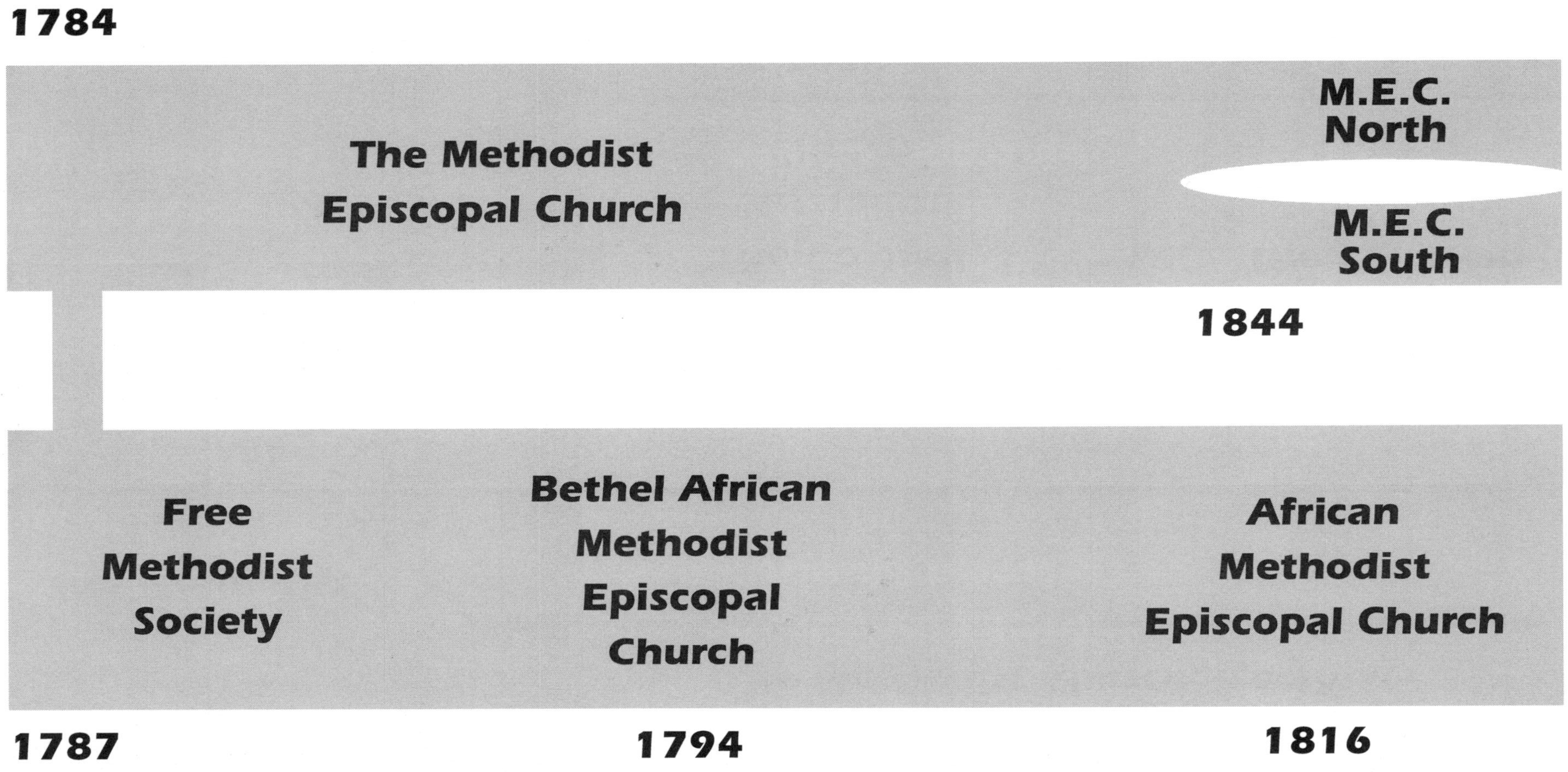

1784

The Methodist Episcopal Church

M.E.C. North

M.E.C. South

1844

1816

African Methodist Episcopal Church

Bethel African Methodist Episcopal Church

1794

Free Methodist Society

1787

Chart 101

The African Methodist Episcopal Church was born out of the perception of racial discrimination at St. George Methodist Church in Philadelphia. Under the leadership of Richard Allen (1760–1831), a former slave, African-Americans formed a church. Ordained by Francis Asbury, Allen later became the church's first bishop. The church boasts over two and a half million members and over six thousand churches.

The Christian Methodist Church

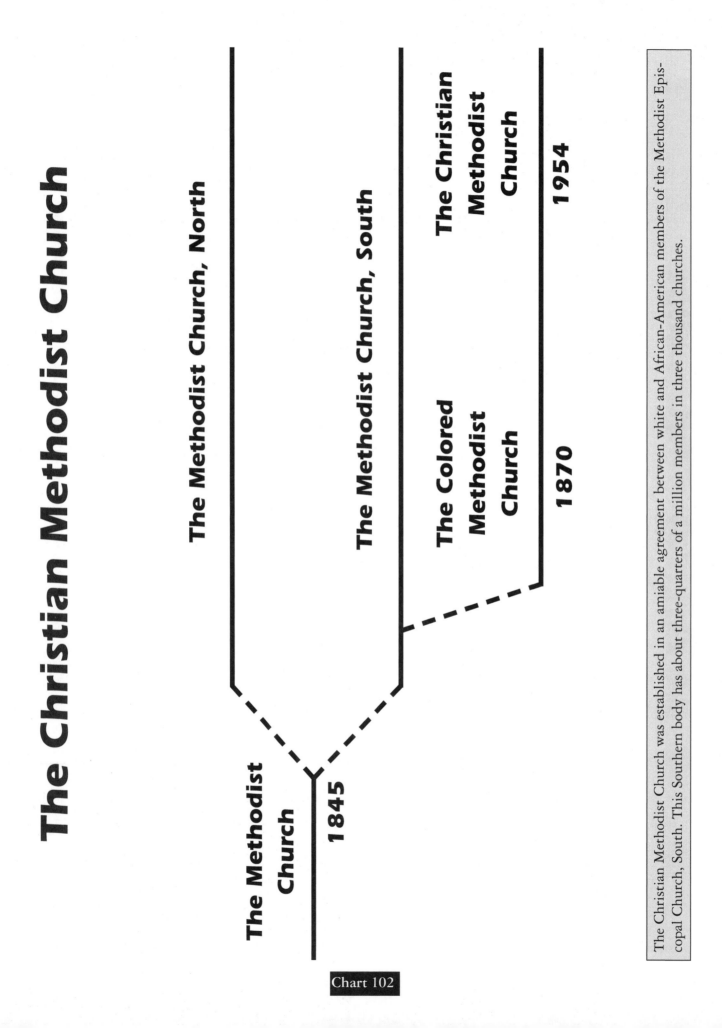

The Methodist Church, North

The Methodist Church, South

The Colored Methodist Church

The Christian Methodist Church

The Methodist Church

1845

1870

1954

Chart 102

The Christian Methodist Church was established in an amiable agreement between white and African-American members of the Methodist Episcopal Church, South. This Southern body has about three-quarters of a million members in three thousand churches.

The Major African-American Baptist Denominations in America

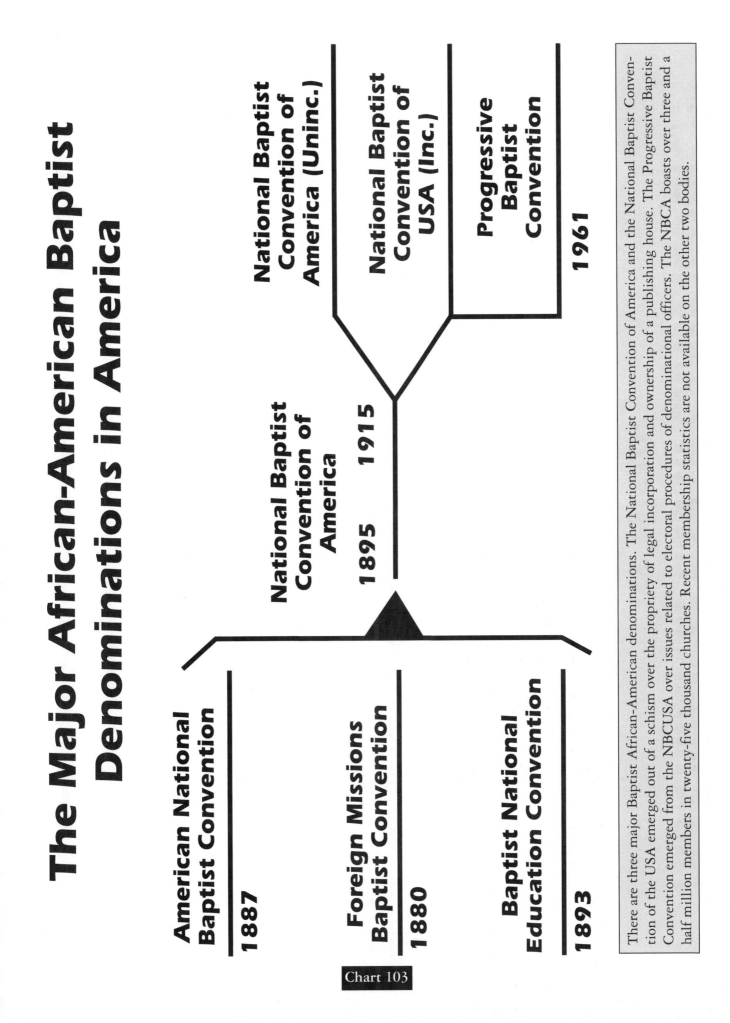

American National Baptist Convention
1887

Foreign Missions Baptist Convention
1880

Baptist National Education Convention
1893

National Baptist Convention of America
1895   1915

National Baptist Convention of America (Uninc.)

National Baptist Convention of USA (Inc.)

Progressive Baptist Convention
1961

Chart 103

There are three major Baptist African-American denominations. The National Baptist Convention of America and the National Baptist Convention of the USA emerged out of a schism over the propriety of legal incorporation and ownership of a publishing house. The Progressive Baptist Convention emerged from the NBCUSA over issues related to electoral procedures of denominational officers. The NBCA boasts over three and a half million members in twenty-five thousand churches. Recent membership statistics are not available on the other two bodies.

The Church of God in Christ (COGIC): Its History

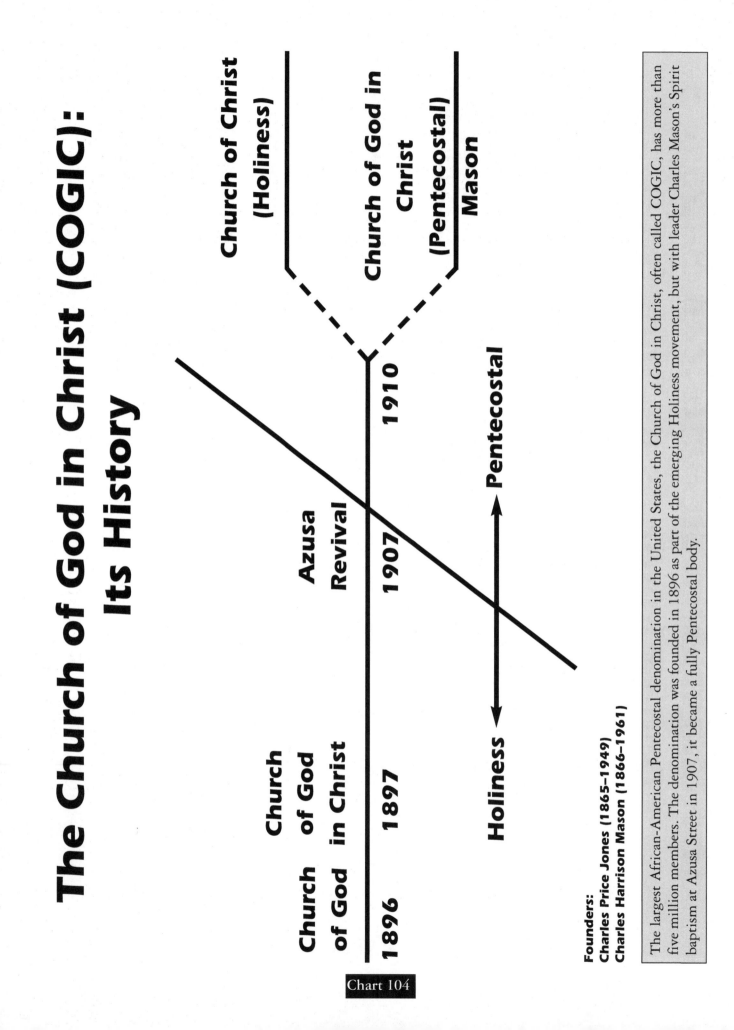

Church of God in Christ

1896 1897

Church of Christ (Holiness)

Azusa Revival

1907

1910

Church of God in Christ (Pentecostal)

Mason

Holiness ↔ Pentecostal

Chart 104

Founders:
Charles Price Jones (1865–1949)
Charles Harrison Mason (1866–1961)

The largest African-American Pentecostal denomination in the United States, the Church of God in Christ, often called COGIC, has more than five million members. The denomination was founded in 1896 as part of the emerging Holiness movement, but with leader Charles Mason's Spirit baptism at Azusa Street in 1907, it became a fully Pentecostal body.

The Charismatic Movements
in America

The History of the Charismatic Movements in America

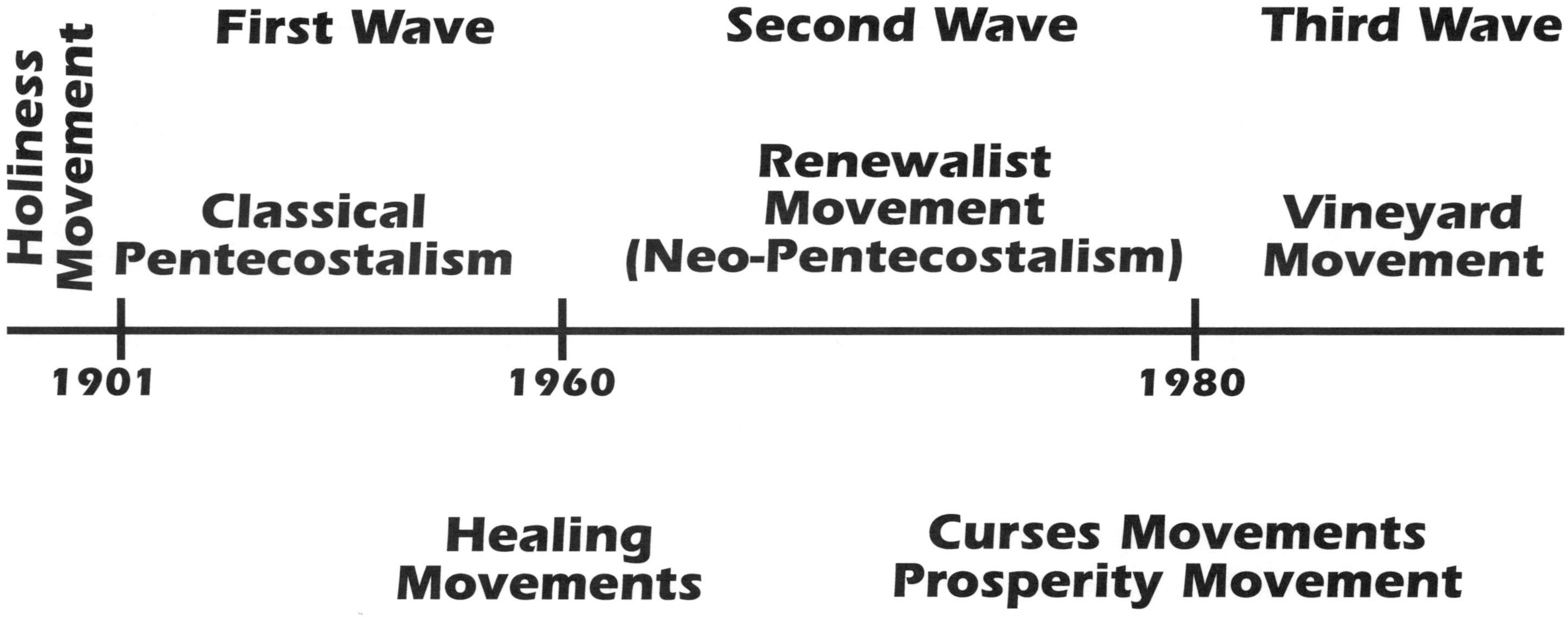

First Wave

Second Wave

Third Wave

Classical Pentecostalism

Renewalist Movement (Neo-Pentecostalism)

Vineyard Movement

Holiness Movement

1901

1960

1980

Healing Movements

Curses Movements
Prosperity Movement

The modern Charismatic movement has progressed through three phases. With early roots in Methodist-Holiness theology, the initial manifestation was Pentecostalism. The healing revivals of the 1940s and 1950s brought a reorientation that culminated in the Charismatic movements of the 1960s and 1970s. The most recent phase has been the Vineyard movement and the variety of movements that emerged from it.

Chart 105

The Charismatic Movements: Shifting Emphases

History

1901   Classic Pentecostalism

1960   Renewalism (Denominationalism)

1990   Restorationism (Latter Rain)

(Kingdom Theology, Positive Confession/Word of Faith, Third Wave)

"The Five-Fold Ministry"
Ephesians 4:11

1940s   Charles Branham
Oral Roberts
Gordon Lindsey
P. G. Hunt

Another way of organizing the history of the Charismatic movement is to think of it as several movements. The Classical Pentecostal movement emerged in the early 1900s and was a separatist movement; the Renewalist movement in the 1960s focused on the reinvigoration of the mainline churches; and the recent Restoration movements emerged with such emphases as prosperity theology, dominion theology, and positive confessionalism. These movements share a common perspective of considering themselves a fulfillment of Joel 2, the Latter Rain, a period of the fuller manifestation of the work of the Spirit.

Chart 106

The Holiness Movement's Emergence from Methodism

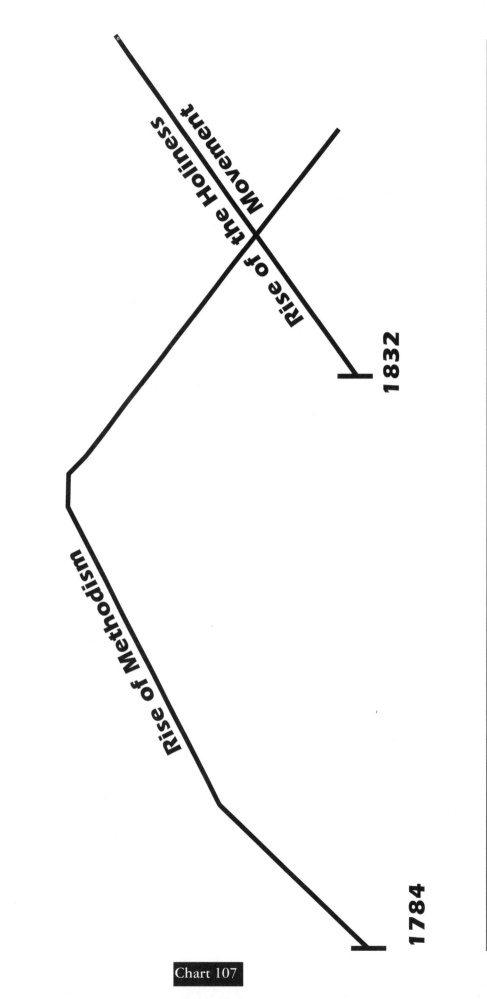

Rise of Methodism

Rise of the Holiness Movement

1784

1832

Chart 107

The context of the rise of the Holiness movement within American Methodism was the rapid reversal of the denomination's growth in the 1830s. Many believed that it was the failure of the church to emphasize a second work of grace that was the cause of the decline.

Holiness Theology:
John Wesley and Sanctification

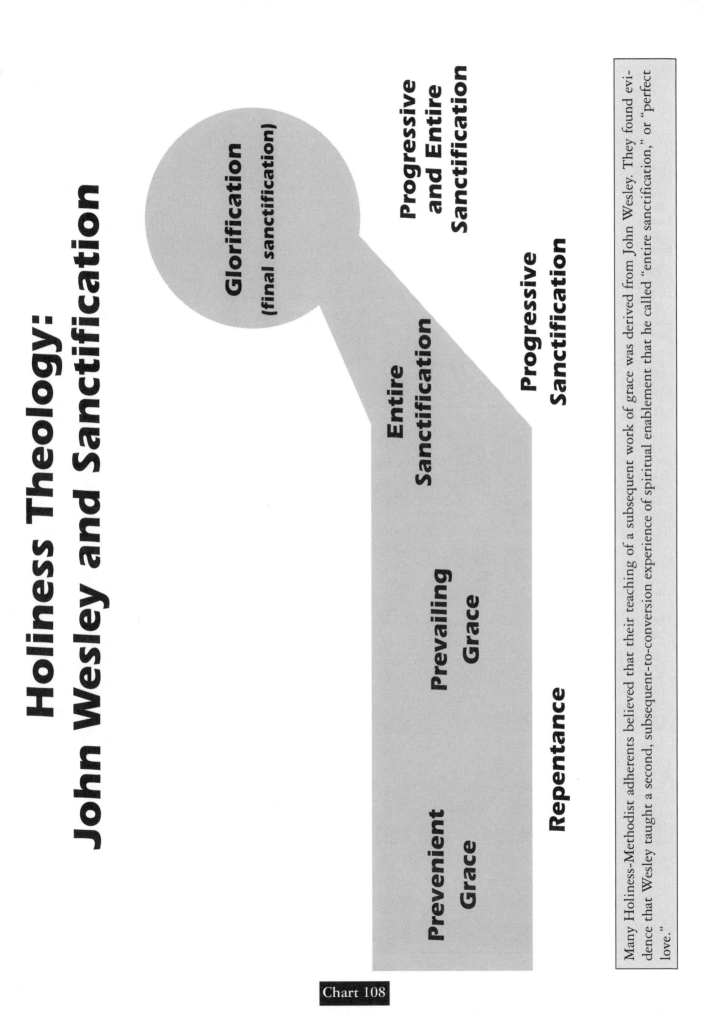

Glorification
(final sanctification)

Progressive and Entire Sanctification

Progressive Sanctification

Entire Sanctification

Prevailing Grace

Repentance

Prevenient Grace

Many Holiness-Methodist adherents believed that their teaching of a subsequent work of grace was derived from John Wesley. They found evidence that Wesley taught a second, subsequent-to-conversion experience of spiritual enablement that he called "entire sanctification," or "perfect love."

Chart 108

The Essence of Holiness Teaching

Salvation by Grace

Sanctification by Surrender (Eradicationism)

Chart 109

The essence of Holiness teaching was that the Christian life has two great moments—conversion to Christ and empowerment through Christ by personal dedication. The second work of grace provided such an infusion of power that victory over sin was an ever-present possibility.

The Rise and Development of Pentecostalism

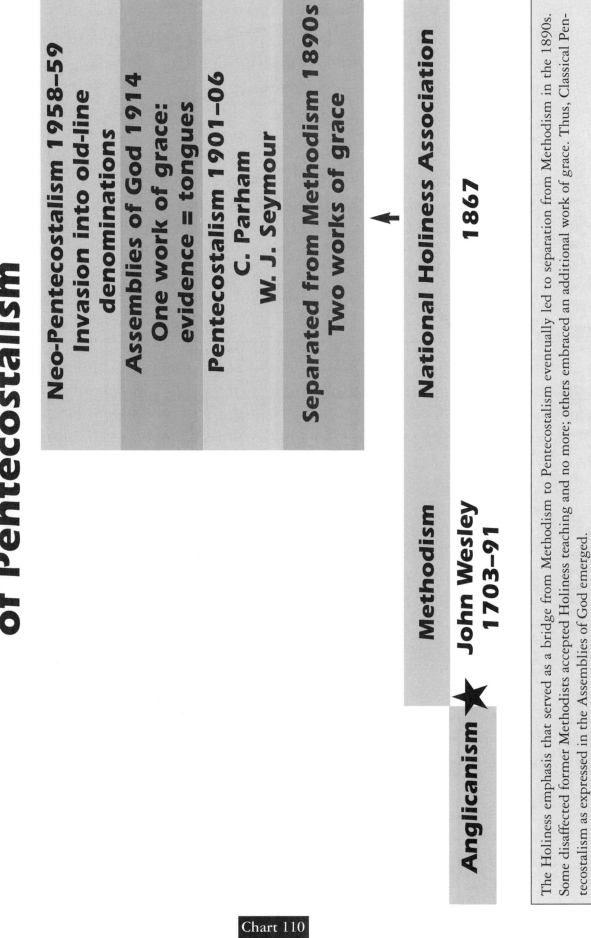

Neo-Pentecostalism 1958–59
Invasion into old-line denominations

Assemblies of God 1914
One work of grace:
evidence = tongues

Pentecostalism 1901–06
C. Parham
W. J. Seymour

Separated from Methodism 1890s
Two works of grace

National Holiness Association
1867

Methodism

★ **John Wesley**
1703–91

Anglicanism

The Holiness emphasis that served as a bridge from Methodism to Pentecostalism eventually led to separation from Methodism in the 1890s. Some disaffected former Methodists accepted Holiness teaching and no more; others embraced an additional work of grace. Thus, Classical Pentecostalism as expressed in the Assemblies of God emerged.

Chart 110

The Church of the Nazarene:
A Church in the Holiness Tradition

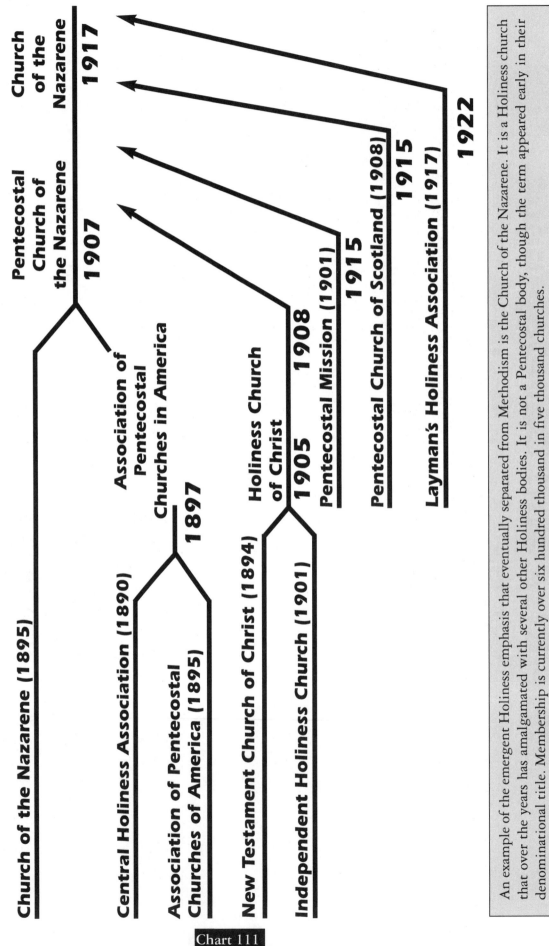

Church of the Nazarene (1895)

Church of the Nazarene

1917

Pentecostal Church of the Nazarene

1907

Association of Pentecostal Churches in America

1897

Central Holiness Association (1890)

Association of Pentecostal Churches of America (1895)

Holiness Church of Christ

1905   1908

New Testament Church of Christ (1894)

Independent Holiness Church (1901)

Pentecostal Mission (1901)

1915

Pentecostal Church of Scotland (1908)

1915

Layman's Holiness Association (1917)

1922

Chart 111

An example of the emergent Holiness emphasis that eventually separated from Methodism is the Church of the Nazarene. It is a Holiness church that over the years has amalgamated with several other Holiness bodies. It is not a Pentecostal body, though the term appeared early in their denominational title. Membership is currently over six hundred thousand in five thousand churches.

The International Pentecostal Holiness Church: A Holiness Church Turned Pentecostal

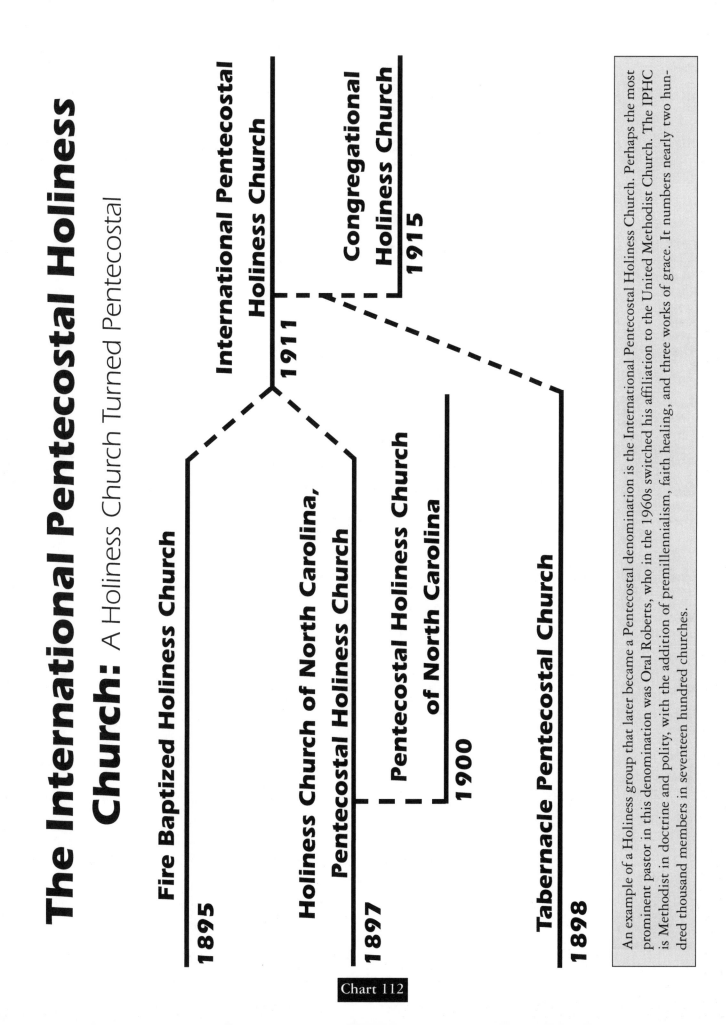

Fire Baptized Holiness Church

1895

Holiness Church of North Carolina,
Pentecostal Holiness Church

1897

Pentecostal Holiness Church
of North Carolina

1900

Tabernacle Pentecostal Church

1898

International Pentecostal
Holiness Church

1911

Congregational
Holiness Church

1915

An example of a Holiness group that later became a Pentecostal denomination is the International Pentecostal Holiness Church. Perhaps the most prominent pastor in this denomination was Oral Roberts, who in the 1960s switched his affiliation to the United Methodist Church. The IPHC is Methodist in doctrine and polity, with the addition of premillennialism, faith healing, and three works of grace. It numbers nearly two hundred thousand members in seventeen hundred churches.

Chart 112

The History of the Church of God Movement

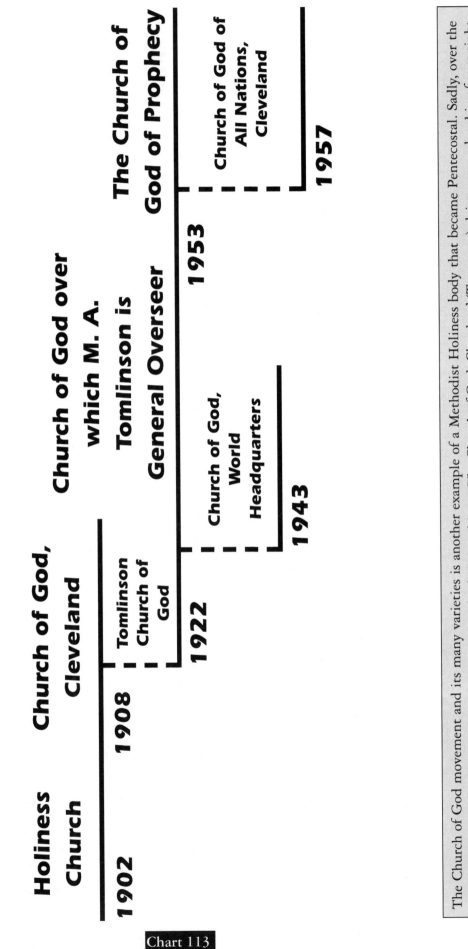

Holiness Church	Church of God, Cleveland		Church of God over which M. A. Tomlinson is General Overseer	The Church of God of Prophecy
		Tomlinson Church of God	Church of God, World Headquarters	Church of God of All Nations, Cleveland
1902	1908	1922	1943	1953 1957

Chart 113

The Church of God movement and its many varieties is another example of a Methodist Holiness body that became Pentecostal. Sadly, over the years, it has experienced a number of controversies leading to schisms. The Church of God, Cleveland (Tennessee) claims a membership of over eight hundred thousand members in six thousand churches.

David Wesley Myland and the Terminology of Classical Pentecostalism

"Be glad then, ye children of Zion, and rejoice in the Lᴏʀᴅ your God: for He hath given you the early rain moderately, and He will cause to come down for you the rain, the early rain and the latter rain in the first month."

Joel 2:23 (KJV)

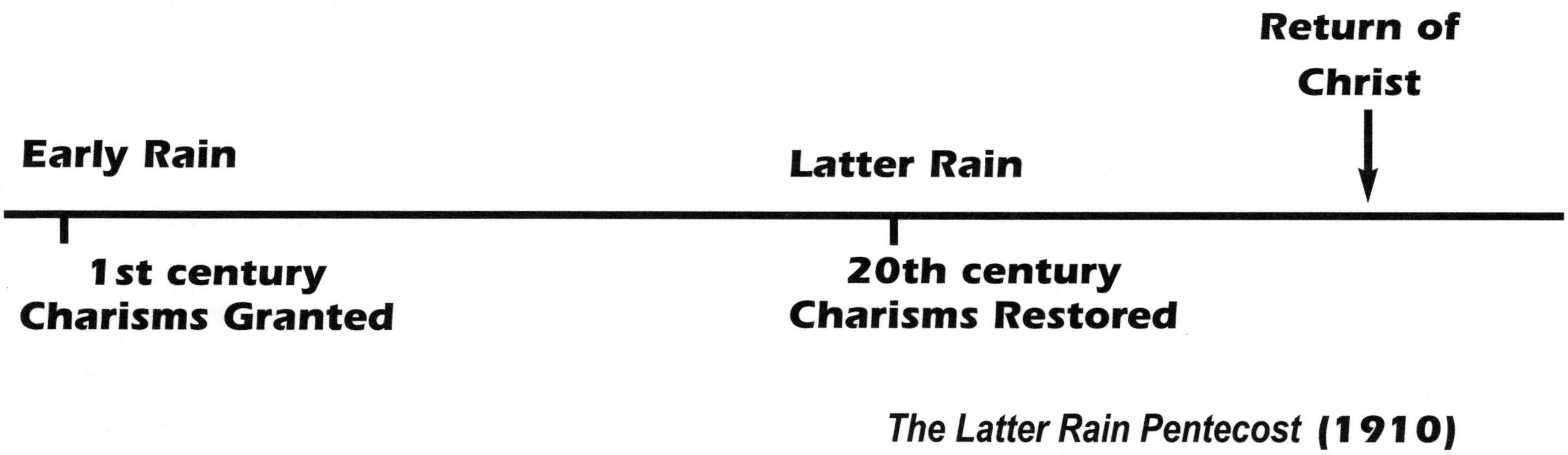

Return of Christ

→

Latter Rain

20th century
Charisms Restored

The Latter Rain Pentecost (1910)

Early Rain

1st century
Charisms Granted

Chart 114

The terminology of the Pentecostal effusion of the Spirit in the Latter Days is found in the writings of David Wesley Myland (1858–1943). He argued that the Joel 2 promise of a former and latter rain was fulfilled in the Spirit's coming upon Peter in Acts 2 and more abundantly in the Latter Rain Revival, as the early Pentecostal movement was called. Myland supported his point by doing a history of rainfall.

Pioneers of Early Pentecostalism

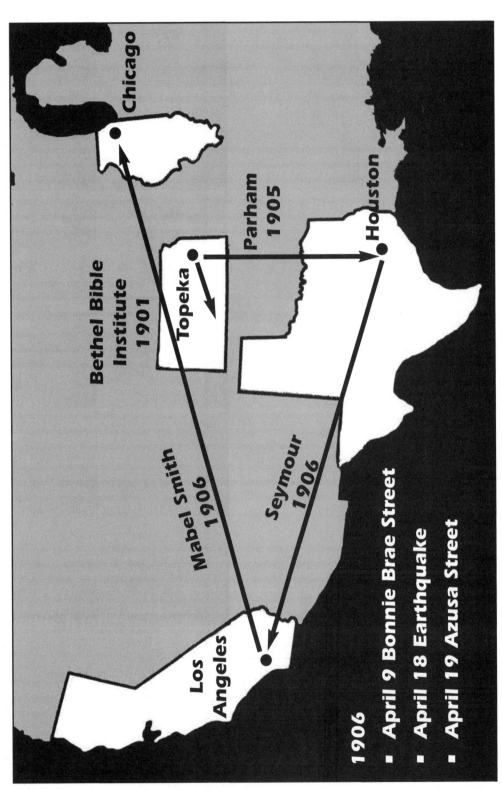

Chicago

Bethel Bible
Institute
1901

Topeka

Parham
1905

Houston

Mabel Smith
1906

Seymour
1906

Los
Angeles

1906
- April 9 Bonnie Brae Street
- April 18 Earthquake
- April 19 Azusa Street

The early pioneers of the Latter Rain or Pentecostal movement were Charles Fox Parham (1879–1927), Agnes Ozman (1870–1937), and William J. Seymour (1870–1922). Parham opened a Bible school in Topeka, Kansas, where the movement began in 1901 (Ozman was one of his students), then opened another school in Houston, Texas, where Seymour accepted the message of a "New Pentecost." Seymour took the teaching to Los Angeles where it became an international movement in the Azusa Revival. Other early centers of growth were Chicago; Dunn, North Carolina; and Oslo, Norway, under the leadership of William Durham, G. B. Cashwell, and Thomas Ball Barrett, respectively.

Chart 115

The Classical Pentecostal
View of Sanctification

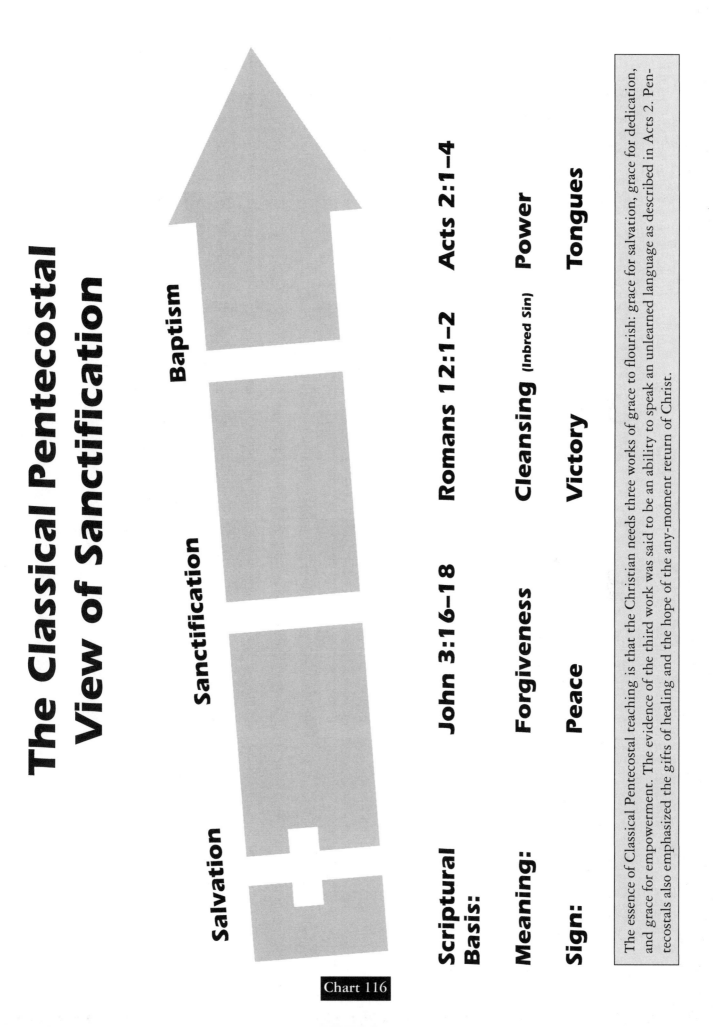

	Salvation	Sanctification	Baptism
Scriptural Basis:	John 3:16–18	Romans 12:1–2	Acts 2:1–4
Meaning:	Forgiveness	Cleansing (Inbred Sin)	Power
Sign:	Peace	Victory	Tongues

The essence of Classical Pentecostal teaching is that the Christian needs three works of grace to flourish: grace for salvation, grace for dedication, and grace for empowerment. The evidence of the third work was said to be an ability to speak an unlearned language as described in Acts 2. Pentecostals also emphasized the gifts of healing and the hope of the any-moment return of Christ.

Chart 116

The "Finished Work" Theory of Pentecostal Sanctification and the Assemblies of God

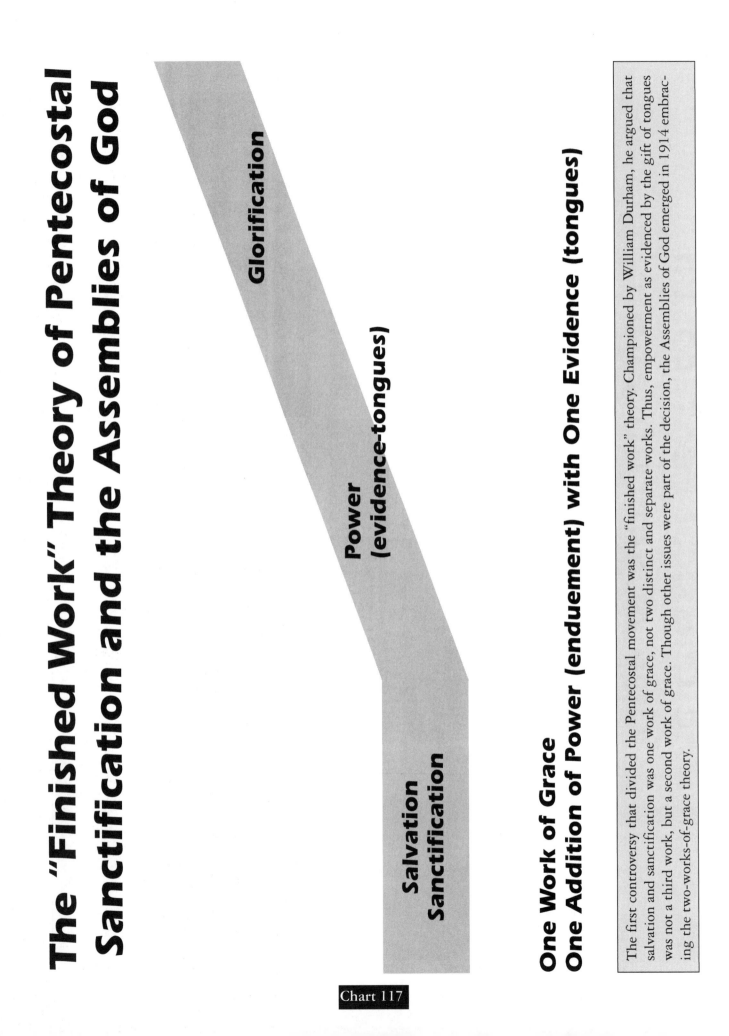

Glorification

Power
(evidence-tongues)

Salvation
Sanctification

One Work of Grace
One Addition of Power (enduement) with One Evidence (tongues)

The first controversy that divided the Pentecostal movement was the "finished work" theory. Championed by William Durham, he argued that salvation and sanctification was one work of grace, not two distinct and separate works. Thus, empowerment as evidenced by the gift of tongues was not a third work, but a second work of grace. Though other issues were part of the decision, the Assemblies of God emerged in 1914 embracing the two-works-of-grace theory.

Chart 117

The Oneness Controversy and the United Pentecostal Church, International

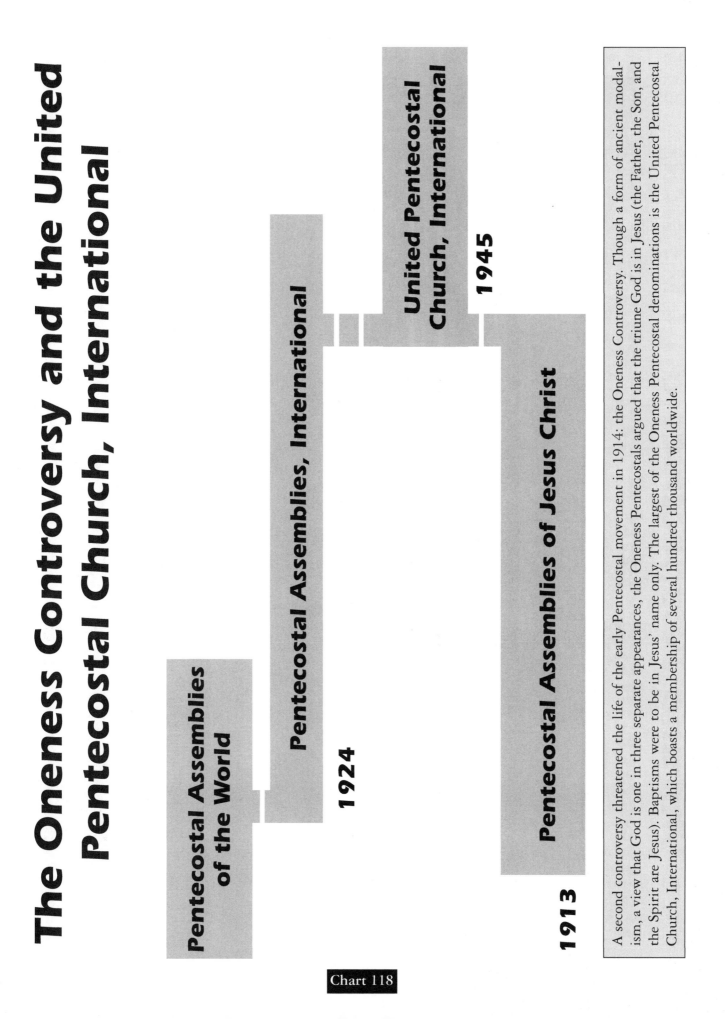

Pentecostal Assemblies of the World

Pentecostal Assemblies, International

1924

United Pentecostal Church, International

1945

Pentecostal Assemblies of Jesus Christ

1913

A second controversy threatened the life of the early Pentecostal movement in 1914: the Oneness Controversy. Though a form of ancient modalism, a view that God is one in three separate appearances, the Oneness Pentecostals argued that the triune God is in Jesus (the Father, the Son, and the Spirit are Jesus). Baptisms were to be in Jesus' name only. The largest of the Oneness Pentecostal denominations is the United Pentecostal Church, International, which boasts a membership of several hundred thousand worldwide.

Chart 118

Shifting Perspectives on Classical Pentecostalism: The Evangelical Embrace

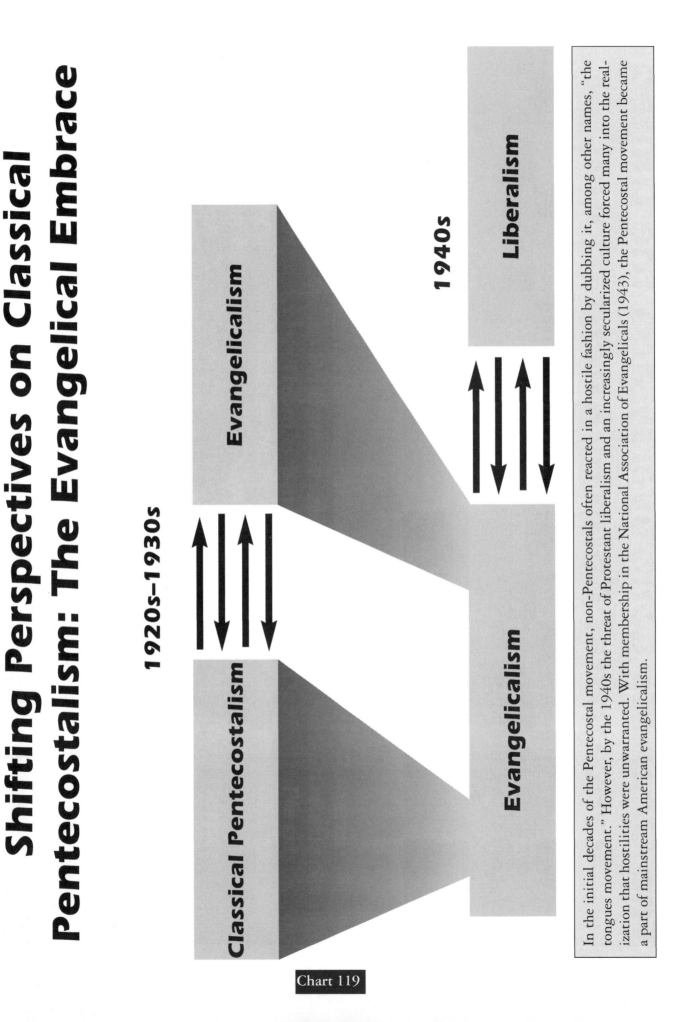

1920s–1930s

Classical Pentecostalism

Evangelicalism

1940s

Evangelicalism

Liberalism

In the initial decades of the Pentecostal movement, non-Pentecostals often reacted in a hostile fashion by dubbing it, among other names, "the tongues movement." However, by the 1940s the threat of Protestant liberalism and an increasingly secularized culture forced many into the realization that hostilities were unwarranted. With membership in the National Association of Evangelicals (1943), the Pentecostal movement became a part of mainstream American evangelicalism.

Chart 119

The Charismatic Renewalist Movement

Holiness Movement	Classical Pentecostalism	Neo-Pentecostalism
	1906	1959
William Boardman	Charles Parham	Oral Roberts
Robert Smith	William Seymour	Demos Shakarian
Hannah Smith	Thomas Barrett	David DuPlessis
R. A. Torrey	Aimee McPherson	Kathryn Kuhlman
Phoebe Palmer	W. H. Durham	Ralph Wilkerson
A. B. Simpson		Michael Harper
Joseph H. Smith		Dennis Bennett
Charles Finney		Edward O'Connor
		Jean Stone

Chart 120

In the 1960s, a neo-Pentecostal or Renewalist movement emerged from within mainline Protestantism and the Roman Catholic Church. Eschewing the more narrow, moralistic, and separatistic traits as well as the rigid theological expectancies of the older Pentecostal movement, the new movement promoted a renewal and uniting of Christendom around a personal, charismatic experience with God.

The Baptism of the Spirit and Charismatic Renewalism

Confirmation

Meaning:
Actualization of
Spirit Baptism

Evidence:
A Charism

Work of Grace:
Released (the Fruit)

Initiation

Meaning:
Spirit Baptism

Evidence:
Water Baptism

Work of Grace:
Given (the Seed)

The mainline Protestant denominations as well as Roman Catholic churches were able to adapt the Pentecostal message to their particular settings. The Holy Spirit was more overtly connected to the initiatory rite of water baptism and its fullest manifestation to a subsequent exercise of spiritual gifts.

Chart 121

John Wimber, The Vineyard Movement, and Spiritual Effectiveness

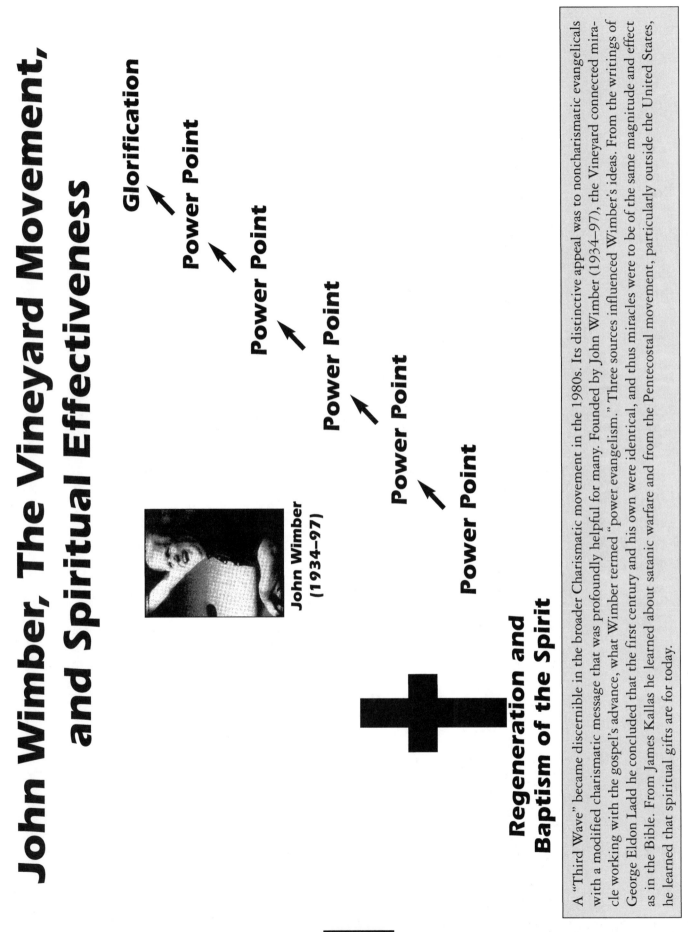

Glorification

Power Point

Power Point

Power Point

Power Point

Power Point

John Wimber
(1934–97)

**Regeneration and
Baptism of the Spirit**

A "Third *Wave*" became discernible in the broader Charismatic movement in the 1980s. Its distinctive appeal was to noncharismatic evangelicals with a modified charismatic message that was profoundly helpful for many. Founded by John Wimber (1934–97), the Vineyard connected miracle working with the gospel's advance, what Wimber termed "power evangelism." Three sources influenced Wimber's ideas. From the writings of George Eldon Ladd he concluded that the first century and his own were identical, and thus miracles were to be of the same magnitude and effect as in the Bible. From James Kallas he learned about satanic warfare and from the Pentecostal movement, particularly outside the United States, he learned that spiritual gifts are for today.

Chart 122

Changing Emphases within the Vineyard Movement

Signs, Wonders, and Power Evangelism

Latter Rain Revival

Signs, Wonders, and Power Evangelism

The Kansas City Prophets Movement

The Toronto Blessing Movement

1994

1988

1996

Increased signs

Decreased signs

1982

1986

Paul Cain
Mike Bickle

Chart 123

The Vineyard movement has evidenced phases since its inception. It began by emphasizing miracles as a powerful tool in evangelism and spiritual growth, and then the emphasis shifted to prophecy (the Kansas City Prophets movement of the 1980s) and ecstatic experiences (the Toronto Blessing movement of the mid-1990s, where "slaying in the Spirit" became a slaying in holy laughter). In the later years of Wimber's leadership, the movement moved back to the original emphasis on "signs and wonders."

THE POSTMODERN PERIOD OF AMERICAN CHURCH HISTORY

The Crisis in American Evangelicalism:

A Movement Caught in Change

"Evangelicalism indeed is in the midst of a crisis."
(Stanley Grenz, Revisioning Evangelical Theology)

The Modern Era
1750

Chart 124

Reason/Experience
Progress
Optimism
Science
Individualism
Pragmatism

The Postmodern Era
1980

Imagination
Disorder
Fragmentation
Technology
Pleasure
Uncertainty

The modern era was based on Newtonian science that emphasized experiment and predictability; it was empirical and rational. However, the scientific base of the postmodern era is quantum physics; unpredictability has replaced certainty. American evangelicalism is in a state of flux as it attempts to come to grips with life in a world that rejects the assumptions of the Enlightenment which shaped how the Christian faith was presented. The current crisis is one of finding ourselves in a strange "new world" of values and assumptions.

The Church Growth Movement

Missions Observations

Stateside Application

Institute of Church Growth Eugene, OR

Institute of Church Growth Fuller Seminary Pasadena, CA

Overseas principles applied: the rational marketing phase

1933

1965

1985

Aware that the prosperity of churches requires careful study and effort, a movement emerged to make it a goal of intense analysis. This movement has had and continues to have a huge impact on churches worldwide in developing marketing strategies for church growth.

Postmodernism and Authority

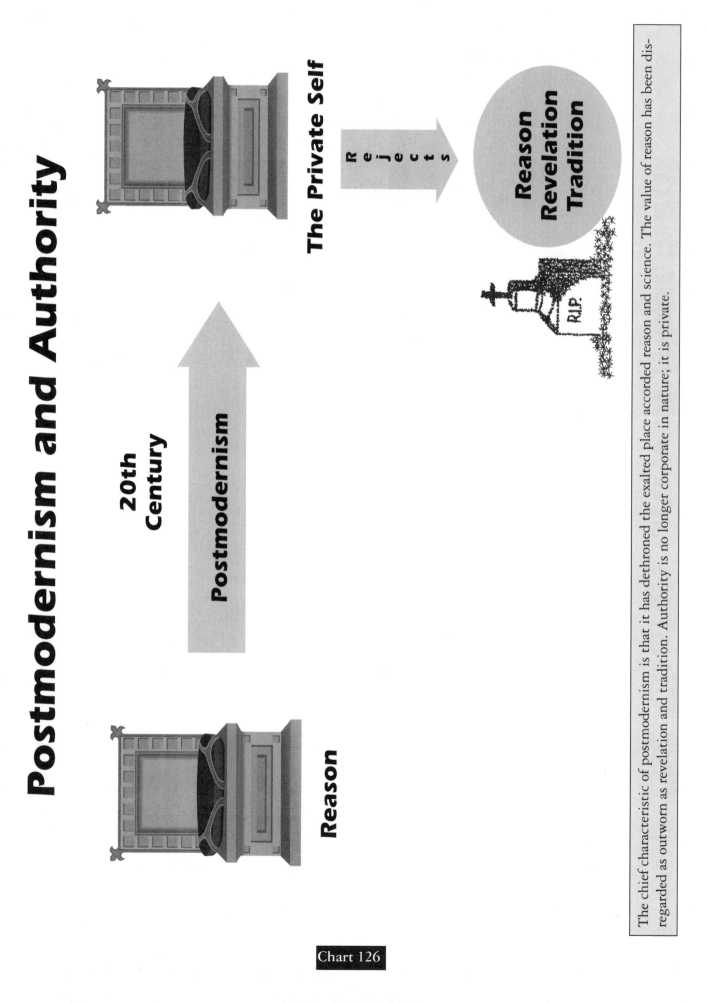

Reason

20th Century

Postmodernism

The Private Self

Rejects

Reason
Revelation
Tradition

R.I.P.

The chief characteristic of postmodernism is that it has dethroned the exalted place accorded reason and science. The value of reason has been disregarded as outworn as revelation and tradition. Authority is no longer corporate in nature; it is private.

Chart 126

The Symbol of Postmodernism

"The condom is the best symbol for this declining stage of modern consciousness. No technological artifice better tells the story of autonomous individualism, narcissistic hedonism, and reductive naturalism than this flimsy rubber sheath. There are some runner-up candidate symbols of the joint ironic success and failure of modern technology—maybe the hypodermic needle, Valium, smart bombs, chlorofluorocarbons, or DDT. But none says more about what modernity promises and delivers than the supposedly leak-prone condom (with its unreassuring, 80 percent 'success' with educated use)."

Thomas Oden, "On Not Whoring After the Spirit of the Age"
in No God But God

The essence of a postmodern approach to life is self-preoccupation and self-centeredness. Nowhere is selfish irresponsibility more evident than in our deepest social relationships.

Chart 127

Postmodernity and the "Self"

"The self-esteem theory predicts that only those who feel good about themselves will do well—which is supposedly why all students need self-esteem—but in fact feeling good about yourself may simply make you over-confident, narcissistic, and unable to work hard....

"In this world, we will perpetually be somewhat sick, mentally and physically. We do not need to be psychologically sound to know and love Christ—for which we should be profoundly grateful."

Paul Vitz, "Leaving the Psychology Behind"

in No God But God

"Within America, the past generation has witnessed a titanic double shift: from the more traditional emphasis on individualism, with its accompanying concern with majority rule, to the more recent emphasis on tribalism, with its accompanying concern with minority rights."

Os Guinness, "More Victimized Than Thou"

in No God But God

Ours has become a world in which self-interest determines the validity of action. In the Enlightenment, the worldview shifted from the Bible and supernatural religion to rationality and natural religion. In the wake of its failure, it seems that postmoderns have nowhere to turn but the inner self.

Chart 128

The Relationship of Secular Humanism to New Age Philosophy

Critical Analysis

1. **Need to change**

2. **Inadequacy of solutions**

Solution

1. **Appeal to a forgotten tradition**

2. **Promise of hope**

In the waning decades of the twentieth century, the demise of the Enlightenment worldview was heralded by the emergence of secular humanism. The spiritual counterpart of secularism was the New Age movement. Whereas secularism offered stinging criticism of traditional spirituality, New Age philosophy presented an alternative.

Chart 129

Secular Humanism and
New Age Teachings Compared

	Secular Humanism	**New Age Movement**
Nature of God:	Nonexistent	Impersonal/amoral
Nature of Reality:	Material monism (matter/energy)	Mystical monism (spirit/consciousness)
Basis of Knowledge:	Rational	Contemplative
Nature of Man:	Product of evolution	Spiritual being
Nature of the Human Dilemma:	Ignorance of the external world	Ignorance of internal potential
Locus of the Human Solution:	Reason/technology	Consciousness (self)
Death:	End of existence	Illusion, reincarnation
Ethics:	Situational/relative	Situational/relative
History:	Linear, chance	Cyclical
Religion:	Superstition	Syncretism
Christ:	Moral teacher	An avatar (guru-god)

Chart 130

Secular humanism and New Age theory stand in marked contrast to each other. The former is materialist in nature; the latter seeks to fill the void in the human soul caused by the absence of spiritual meaning in a world that often defies understanding and purpose.

The Premises and Denials of New Age Teaching

	Premises	Denials
Monism	"All is one"; "all the same"	Denial of divine creation and created plurality. Rejection of all dualisms.
Pantheism	"All is god"	Denial of a personal God. Rejection of creator/creaturely distinctives.
Anthrotheism	"Man is god"	Denial of human finiteness. Rejection of human uniqueness (image of God).
Cosmic Consciousness	"Man creates reality"; "The messiah within"	Denial of human limitation. Rejection of the need for divine grace.
Religious Syncretism	"The religions are equally useful"	Denial of the uniqueness of Christianity. Rejection of Christ's claims.
Cosmic Evolution Consciousness	"The end of history is planetary consciousness"	Denial of a divine control over history. Rejection of a divine eschaton.

Chart 131

New Age advocates believe that the world is deeply spiritual and is far more than just what the senses can experience. Though Christianity would not argue these points, New Age is at its root a conscious rejection of Christian values and teachings. It borrows heavily from Hinduism (pantheism, karma, reincarnation).

Modern and Postmodern Views of Truth

Modern	Postmodern
Objective	Subjective
Scientific	Mystic
Empirical	Experiential
Individual	Communitarian

The impact of postmodern cultural values on the mission of the church is neither all evil nor all good. The modern assumption of objective truth acquired solely through reason slighted the necessity of divine revelation. Christian faith is neither rational nor irrational; it is suprarational. It confesses to truth beyond our senses. Further, postmodernism should help us to see afresh the value of personal testimony in witnessing to the Christian faith.

Chart 132

Alvin Toffler and the Future

"We live in the final irretrievable crisis of industrialization.
And as the industrial age passes into history, a new age is born."

	Agrarian Age 1700	Industrial Age 1956	Informational Age
Sounds:	Rooster	Factory Whistle	Computer
Energy:	Renewable	Nonrenewable (fossil fuels)	Diversity/ Renewability
		Nuclear	Aggregate
Family:	Extended		
Characteristics:	Individualism Community	Standardization Specialization Synchronization Centralization Linearization Mechanization	Decentralization Deurbanization
Economics:	Production and Consumer United	Production and Consumer Separated	Production and Consumer Connected

Chart 133

ZondervanCharts
Charts of Ancient and Medieval Church History
Book I

The first in a series of three books, *Charts of Ancient and Medieval Church History* provides a powerful visual tool for understanding the historic foundations on which contemporary Christians rest. From geography, to theology, to doctrines both orthodox and heretical, to key figures and movements across the centuries, the broad, comprehensive scope of early church history comes across simply, clearly, and with impact.

Divided into two sections—Ancient and Medieval—this book covers the first 1,500 years of church history with nearly 160 charts, diagrams, and maps grouped under numerous subdivisions. A sampler of subdivisions and specific charts includes:

Introductions: Church History in a Nutshell
Prominent Cities
The Setting of the Church
The Life of Jesus Christ
The Age of the Earliest Church Fathers
The Age of the Apologists
Essential Components of Gnosticism
The Creed of Chalcedon
Pelagius and Augustine Compared
The Rise of Episcopacy and Papacy in the Church
The Emergence of the Roman Catholic Church
The Rise of the Islamic Faith
The Division of the Church: West and East
The Crusades
Scholasticism
The Church on the Eve of the Reformation

The PowerPoint® CD-ROM supplied with this book gives instructors an ideal tool for classroom and group presentations. *Charts of Ancient and Medieval Church History* will help Christians not only develop a firm grasp on the rich legacy of their faith, but understand how it influences the church today and their own lives as believers.

Softcover: 0-310-23316-X

Pick up a copy today at your favorite bookstore!

ZONDERVAN™
GRAND RAPIDS, MICHIGAN 49530 USA
WWW.ZONDERVAN.COM

ZondervanCharts
Charts of Reformation and Enlightenment Church History
Book 2

Major Schisms in the First Sixteen Centuries • Development of Church Government • Orthodoxy and Unitarianism Compared • Education in Puritan England • Christianity and the American Revolution • Origins of Presbyterians, Baptists, Methodists, and Lutherans

These are just a sample of the charts in this book, designed to provide a visual survey of a key part of our Christian heritage. *Charts of Reformation and Enlightenment Church History* covers the major events, movements, and people from the sixteenth century to the beginning of the nineteenth century. It includes charts of ideas and trends as well as pertinent diagrams.

The book is divided into three primary sections:
• Early Modern Europe and the Reformation (1500 to 1650) • The Rise of Religious Rationalism and the Enlightenment (1650 to 1750) • The Period of British Settlement in North America: The Colonial Period of American Religious History (1600 to 1800)

Within these sections, ninety charts are arranged under seventeen headings:

1. The Background of the Reformation
2. The Lutheran Reformation
3. The Calvinist Reformation
4. The Anabaptist Reformation
5. The English Reformation
6. The Roman Catholic Reformation
7. The Rise of Religious Rationalism
8. The Enlightenment
9. The Reaction against Creedalism and Rationalism: Pietism
10. Backgrounds of American Religious History
11. Congregationalists
12. Baptists
13. Presbyterians
14. Methodists
15. Other Groups
16. The Great Awakening
17. Religion and the American Revolution

This clear, well-organized reference includes a PowerPoint® CD-ROM for using the eye-catching graphics in a variety of settings.

Softcover: 0-310-23317-8

Pick up a copy today at your favorite bookstore!

Zondervan Charts
Chronological and Background Charts of Church History

Charts provide a synthesis and visual overview of information that helps in teaching, learning, and review. Facts, relationships, parallels, and contrasts are grasped easily and quickly. The eighty-four charts in *Chronological and Background Charts of Church History* provide a summary of key persons, events, dates, and ideas throughout church history—from ancient to modern European and American.

Chapters include:

The Ancient Church (to 478)
The Medieval Church (476–1517)
The Reformation (1517–1648)
The Modern European Church (from 1648)
The American Church (from 1607)

Softcover: 0-310-36281-4

Pick up a copy today at your favorite bookstore!

ZONDERVAN™
GRAND RAPIDS, MICHIGAN 49530 USA
WWW.ZONDERVAN.COM

ZondervanCharts
Timeline Charts of the Western Church

What do the history of the Quaker church and the women's suffrage movement have in common? How did Luther's 95 Theses fit into the wider context of the world in that day? Turn to *Timeline Charts of the Western Church* to find out! *Timeline Charts of the Western Church* is the first comprehensive presentation of the history of the Western Church in a proven and clear timetable format. In three sections, it supplies both summarized and detailed information that students, professors, professionals, and lay persons alike will find valuable and accessible. The main part of the book, modeled after Bernard Grun's *Timetables of History*, organizes in-depth information into four categories:

Theological questions/Issues
People/Events
Wider Culture
Texts

A detailed index supplies enough information to provide a stand-alone resource. Three appendices offer brief overviews that allow the reader to quickly grasp the essentials of different eras in Western Church history.

Softcover: 0-310-22353-9

Pick up a copy today at your favorite bookstore!

ZONDERVAN™

GRAND RAPIDS, MICHIGAN 49530 USA

WWW.ZONDERVAN.COM

ZondervanCharts
Charts of Bible Prophecy

This new addition to the Zondervan*Charts* series of reference tools, *Charts of Bible Prophecy*, helps the student and specialist alike navigate through the many issues, themes, and especially different viewpoints of Bible prophecy. While most books on prophecy deal with the subject from one particular perspective and tend to be dismissive of other views, *Charts of Bible Prophecy* brings the differing views together in an even-handed way for side-by-side comparison.

The 120 charts contained in this volume fall into the following groupings:

- An Introduction to Prophecy
- Hermeneutics and Prophecy
- Fulfillment of Prophecy
- Prophetic Texts
- Systems of Eschatology
- The Rapture and the Second Coming
- The Nation of Israel
- Teaching on the Tribulation
- The Olivet Discourse
- Teaching on the Millennium
- Daniel and Revelation
- Death and Afterlife
- Comparative Eschatology

Softcover: 0-310-21896-9

Pick up a copy today at your favorite bookstore!

ZONDERVAN™
GRAND RAPIDS, MICHIGAN 49530 USA
WWW.ZONDERVAN.COM

ZondervanCharts

Charts of Theology and Biblical Studies

Students as well as laypeople can see how the vast array of interrelated topics and disciplines in theology and biblical studies fit together with this comprehensive collection of charts. A visual tracing of all major areas clarifies the connections and relationships between them.

Softcover: 0-310-21993-0

Charts of Christian Theology and Doctrine

These precise and condensed summaries of concepts and arguments from the fields of historical and systematic theology introduce readers to important terms and positions and their meanings. This handy reference allows students to organize and integrate material learned from a variety of textbooks and in the classroom.

Softcover: 0-310-41661-2

Charts of the Gospels and the Life of Christ

Both students and Bible teachers will find this to be a vital reference tool, study source, and visual aid for New Testament study. It includes extensive charts on the life, ministry, setting, and teachings of Jesus Christ in three main categories: General Background, Chronological Charts, and Thematic Charts.

Softcover: 0-310-22620-1

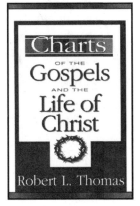

Chronological and Background Charts of the Old Testament

This revised edition of *Chronological and Background Charts of the Old Testament* includes forty-two new charts and eight revised charts. The charts cover historical, literary, archaeological, and theological aspects of the Old Testament, its background, and biblical studies.

Softcover: 0-310-48161-9

Pick up a copy today at your favorite bookstore!